The Politics of Feeling

The Politics of Feeling

Populism, Progressivism, Liberalism

Ben Anderson and Anna J. Secor

Goldsmiths Press

Goldsmiths Press
Deptford Town Hall Goldsmiths, University of London,
New Cross, London SE14 6NW

Copyright © 2025 Goldsmiths Press
First published in 2025 by Goldsmiths Press
Copyright © 2025 Ben Anderson and Anna Secor
Goldsmiths, University of London, New Cross
London SE14 6NW

Printed and bound by Versa Press, USA
Distribution by the MIT Press
Cambridge, Massachusetts, and London, England

The right of the individual contributors to be identified as the authors of this work have been asserted by them in accordance with sections 77 and 78 in the Copyright, Designs and Patents Act 1988.

Every effort has been made to trace copyright holders and to obtain their permission for the use of copyright material. The publisher apologizes for any errors or omissions and would be grateful if notified of any corrections that should be incorporated in future reprints or editions of this book.

All Rights Reserved. No part of this publication may be reproduced, distributed or transmitted in any form or by any means whatsoever without prior written permission of the publisher, except in the case of brief quotations in critical articles and review and certain non-commercial uses permitted by copyright law.

A CIP record for this book is available from the British Library

ISBN 978-1-915983-29-9 Pbk
ISBN 978-1-915983-28-2 Ebk
www.gold.ac.uk/goldsmiths-press

Dedicated to our grandparents who believed in education. To Lorna (1924–2024) and Robert [Bob] Anderson (1926–1997) and Elizabeth (1911–1998) and Wilfrid [Wilf] Gardiner (1906–1983). Elizabeth and Wilf left formal education at 14 and 12, respectively, and Bob at 16 (we think). Lorna studied teacher training between 1942 and 1944 at what was then Goldsmiths College and is now Goldsmiths, University of London. In their different ways, all loved learning and were committed to their children's education. And on the other side of the Atlantic, to Harry Secor (1908–1982), who inspired his son with a love of life and learning. And to Olga (1907–2001) and Michael Jennette (1899–2002), who had little formal education and worked in the factories of Waterbury, Connecticut, yet who sent their daughter and granddaughters to university.

Contents

	Acknowledgements	ix
1	Introduction: The Politics of Feeling in a Conjunctural Crisis	1
2	Populism: Affirmative, Excessive, and Optimistic	49
3	Progressivism: Redemptive, Catastrophic, and Intense	93
4	Liberalism: Defensive, Melancholic, and Boring	131
5	Conclusion: Into the Moving Present	175
	References	191
	Index	211

Acknowledgements

Our thanks to our colleagues at the Department of Geography, Durham University, for creating the inspiring, supportive, and often fun intellectual environment that has made this book possible, and the students on our Level 3 modules Neoliberal Life and Politics and Space, where we first tried out many of the ideas in this book. We are grateful to many who have directly or atmospherically buoyed and inspired us in this project, including Peter Adey, Ash Amin, Jen Bagelman, Andrew Baldwin, Harriet Bulkeley, Rachel Carr, Angharad Closs-Stephens, Rebecca Coleman, Jonny Darling, Alex Densmore, Jeremy Gilbert, Kevin Grove, Paul Harrison, Adam Holden, Sarah Knuth, Jaeyeon Lee, Jess Linz, Lauren Martin, Cheryl McEwan, Colin McFarlane, Hannah Morgan, Aya Nassar, Marijn Nieuwenhuis, George Packer, Joe Painter, Josh Radner, Victoria Ridgway, Amy Robson, Laura Secor, Helen Wilson, and Vickie Zhang – none of whom is in the least responsible for what we have written here. We'd also like to thank the reviewers of this manuscript for their insight and enthusiasm, and Sarah Kember, Ellen Parnavelas, Angela Thompson, and the designers of the front cover for their support.

Chapter 2 includes an edited and expanded version of parts of Anderson B. & Secor, A. (2022) 'Propositions on right-wing populism: Available, excessive, optimistic'. Political Geography, 96, 102608, reproduced with permission of Elsevier.

1
Introduction: The Politics of Feeling in a Conjunctural Crisis

Introduction: Change?

The UK Labour Party's contentless slogan at the 2024 General Election – "Change" – tried to express a public mood that had found multiple political forms since the 2008 financial crisis. From Brexit's "take back control" to Bernie Sanders' "change you can believe in", or Trump's "make America Great again" and Black Lives Matter's demand for future justice, "change" existed as a demand for something, perhaps anything, different to the present impasse. In Labour's hands, the promise of a rupture or reset was articulated with the rehabilitation of the not-very-new neoliberal promises of "growth" and "opportunity". By contrast, the conservatives' flailing campaign invoked the insecurity of the future and the stability of their "clear plan" that was apparently working to secure a better future. Into a scene seemingly characterised by little but disaffection, the spectre or promise of right-wing populism reared up once again, with Nigel Farage returning to electoral politics and pronouncing the 2024 election to be the "immigrant election". Meanwhile, in a US presidential debate, Donald J. Trump and Joe Biden bickered about who was the better golfer in the breaths between asserting that each other was a profound threat to the very future of America. Their golfing argument soon became subject to online parodies, rivalling the short-lived fame of "Hawk Tuah" girl. Some days later back in the UK, as the US appeared consumed by the frailty of President Biden, the leader of the

Liberal Democrats, Ed Davey, was bungie jumping, shouting "Vote Liberal Democrats" as he hurtled towards the earth.

The present from which we finish writing *The Politics of Feeling* in early summer 2024 will soon disappear, with most of the above slogans, scenes, and stunts long forgotten. Others will linger on as portents and promises, depending on political attachment and disposition. But in the mixing of the absurd and deeply dangerous, in the intimacy of boredom with exuberance, in the coexistence of desires for change with the return of the same, this slice of life exemplifies the strange turbulence of the extended impasse that has marked politics after 2008.

The Politics of Feeling is an intervention in how we understand this political impasse in the UK and the US in the period since the 2008 financial crisis. We demonstrate how, in these two countries today, politics is motivated and played out through collective political feelings. If the second half of the 20th century saw the defeat and exhaustion of fascism and socialism, what remained of ideological certainty in democracies such as the UK and the US ran aground in the wake of the 2008 financial crisis. Our contention is that today's competing political forms of *right-wing populism, left progressivism, and contemporary liberalism* are best understood (and critiqued) not as ideologies per se but in terms of the politics of feeling.[1]

---

[1] These are not the only three available sites of political attachment. Conservativism, environmentalism, and a more traditional and revolutionary leftism all come to mind as important political–affective forces today. But more than this, there are any number of structures of feeling, some of which are not yet coherent or even nameable. Populism, progressivism, and liberalism are particularly salient for affective politics in the US and the UK today, and entwined in interesting ways, but are not exhaustive of either contemporary politics or political feeling.

Rather than primarily functioning as coherent programmes of political thought, values, and policy imperatives, today these political forms work by distributing attachment and intensity, operating as collections of rallying points, provocations to outrage, sites of exhilaration or enjoyment, and modes of political performance. This is not to say that there are no political programmes attached to them, but it is to delve into how these political formations work affectively – that is, through feelings – to differentiate and organise political contestation within these two Western democratic societies in our current moment.

We focus on the politics of feeling in a context where claims abound about the overcharged mood of the post-2008 present, with stories of strong feelings and dramatic passions characterising so many public accounts of politics in the UK and the US, whether figured in terms of anger, resentment, and outrage or through attention to burnout, stress, and other affects of frenzy. For others, cynicism and discontent appear to be the signature affects of a fraught, divided public. These claims are in their own terms compelling, but they tend to reduce political forms to a symptom of some wider mood that then comes to characterise the present. Rather than positing a shared mood, in *The Politics of Feeling*, we analyse today's dominant political forms – and the figures, events, and movements that compose them – as differentiated affective responses to the contemporary uncertainty that is unevenly distributed across class, race, gender, and other differences in the US and the UK.

At a time when national institutions appear weakened, economies are stuttering or folding in on themselves, and threats of climate emergency and other catastrophes figure upon a near horizon, the affective appeal of political formations matters as much or more than how they function as a coherent set of ideas. Right-wing populism, progressivism, and liberalism each make available distinctive ways of feeling. By orienting attachments and linking together sites of collective feeling, they all promise (in different ways, to different people) an exit from the impasse of the present and a resolution to the uncertainty that is simultaneously the affective condition for their (re)emergence (for our use of the term "attachment", see Anderson, 2023). These "structures of feeling" (as we conceptualise them, following Raymond Williams) are therefore best understood as modes of distributing, or making differentially available, political intensities within the contemporary conjuncture.

Our intervention is substantive but also theoretical. Inspired by the academic interest in affect over the past twenty years, the book advocates for and performs a practice of diagnostic critique orientated to how conjunctures feel and are sensed. It does so by returning to Williams' (1977) concept of "structures of feeling", placing it alongside other recent work on racialised affect, and finding in it a way of staying with how political forms gather up or 'arrange' feelings and atmospheres (Seigworth and Pedwell, 2023: 13). *The Politics of Feeling*'s focus on the US and the UK allows us to trace out populist, progressive, and liberal feelings in the wake of the collapse, in both these societies, of the expectations that ideologies of capitalist modernism and liberal democracy had fostered, and neoliberalism had, for a time, drawn on for political legitimacy. Bringing these two contexts into the same frame sheds light on how the scenes and patterns of political intensity emitting from the US and the UK diffractively interact to produce troughs and peaks of populist, progressive, and liberal political intensity.

Why these two countries rather than one or the other, or these two rather than two others, or this transatlantic sphere rather than the world in its entirety? Our choice to analyse the affective present across UK and US contexts is shaped both by our own positionalities and by what we perceive as a shared but differentiated sphere of political ideology, performance, and feeling across these contexts. This is apparent in how political rhetoric and culture circulates between the two societies and yet may land quite differently (something we illustrate multiply in the chapters that follow). At times, what crystallises in one context reverberates and becomes a different sort of political-affective force in the other (for example, Brexit in 2016 or Trump's win in 2024). Across our chapters and our propositions, the US and the UK are not always equally involved. A proposition may arise from scenes that are more vivid at one site than the other in a particular moment. Considering this dynamism and contingency, our aim in this book is neither to create static, local images nor to suggest that there is a universal or global form to any of these structures of feeling. Our analysis is of scenes and moments that are not geo-historically free-floating but are also not tied down into one determinant national or trans-national narrative; they are contingent and momentary, their attraction and intensity shifting and differentiating, changing and even sometimes dissolving before the ink is dry.

As a prelude to our analysis of populism, progressivism, and liberalism as structures of feeling unfolding in the US and the UK, we begin with a return to the work of Stuart Hall to deepen our characterisation of the post 2008 present as an unfinished "conjunctural crisis" marked by the fraying hegemony of neoliberal logics and ideals. Centring the turbulence of formal politics over the past sixteen years, we track the emergence of all kinds of morbid symptoms and (pre)emergent heralds of different futures. We then elaborate on the concept of structures of feeling, summarising it via engagement with Raymond Williams and the problem of ideology, while also developing a concern for structures of feeling as differentiated and differentiating. Next, we articulate three tendencies that make up the conjunctural crisis: *spreading and intensifying precariousness, the cancellation of "the future", and the digitally mediated present.* In different ways, each political form (populism, progressivism, and liberalism) responds to, enacts, and refracts these tendencies. They offer ways of making sense and living amid them. As well as summarising the propositions that compose each chapter, our final section discusses the challenges of writing from the present and justifies the mode through which we diagnose populism, progressivism, and liberalism as structures of feeling – by offering contestable propositions.

Conjunctural Crisis

As I see it, history moves from one conjuncture to another rather than being an evolutionary flow. And what drives it forward is usually a crisis, when the contradictions that are always at play in any historical moment are condensed, or, as Althusser said, "fuse in a ruptural unity". Crises are moments of potential change, but the nature of their resolution is not given. (Stuart Hall in Hall and Massey (2010): 57)

We diagnose the affective appeal of populism, progressivism, and liberalism from within a still unfolding conjunctural crisis. A settlement inaugurated at the end of the Cold War and defined by the becoming hegemonic of neoliberal ideas and extension of neoliberal logics has been unravelling. Ruptured by the 2008 financial crisis, the ending of the settlement is expressed in the intensity of debates about whether neoliberalism has ended, lives on zombie-like, or is becoming something new. That something is changing and something new might be emerging is also felt in the proliferation of proper names for whatever today's formation might be – zombie capitalism, zombie neoliberalism, authoritarian neoliberalism, and so on.

How this crisis will be resolved is still not given, to echo Hall's words that still hold some sixteen years later. In the meantime, the present is overfull with morbid and other symptoms.

Like Hall and Massey, we date the advent of the conjunctural crisis to the 2008 financial crisis, an event of rupture and disclosure the long aftermath of which we are still experiencing some sixteen years later. Beginning as an event of market failure, revelatory of the dominance of financialisation to neoliberal capitalism, the event was, from around 2010, governed and narrated globally as a catastrophic failure of the state (see Blyth, 2013; Mirowski, 2013). Early protests against the inequalities of financialisation, principally the Occupy movement, faded, in part because of intense state and ideological repression. Yet the affective force of phrases invented in the Occupy movement such as "the 1 per cent" still linger in the political unconscious, finding new distorted expression in the older populist vocabulary of "elites". Blaming the profligacy of the too extravagant, wasteful state for the financial crisis revived and intensified the state-phobia that accompanies neoliberal reason and logics (Foucault, 2008). This state-phobia became the affective condition for the reduction in both the material resources of the (local) state and its promises that compose austerity. Amplifying the long-term material impacts of the collapse of the Fordist-Keynesian settlement since the late 1970s, including widening inequality (Piketty, 2013), austerity's material legacies have been disastrous, leading to collapsing living standards, worsening health outcomes, and a crumbling public sphere in the UK. In the US, the once dominant middle-class shrinks while life prospects for young and working-class people contract, health outcomes bifurcate, and political polarisation is the most ominous affliction of the public sphere.

Governing through austerity in the 2010s happened alongside emergent and residual protean desires for change. These subsequently found expression in both left and right political events and movements. One intense expression was the emergence of left populism in the realm of formal politics, for example, through the unexpected election of Jeremy Corbyn as Labour Party leader in 2015 and Bernie Sanders' campaign for the 2016 Democratic Party presidential nomination.

But the most immediate, visceral form the unravelling of this settlement took was a series of events in the political realm from 2015 that punctured the confidence of the liberal "centre" and were felt with disorientating shock by some and welcome surprise by others. "Brexit" and the 2016 election of Donald Trump both expressed intense discontent with some aspect of the present, together with the presence of some kind of lurking desire for change, refracted through time loops of restorative nostalgia articulated in bellicose nationalist projects and inseparable from the restoration of a whiteness felt as newly precarious. "Make America Great Again" and "Take Back Control" both promised a restoration of something lost but also the felt agency of "making" and "taking" in the midst of impersonal, global forces. Nationalist optimism organised around maintaining the promises and inheritance of whiteness coexisted with something more nihilistic, a desire simply to break with the here and now, to try something different, whether whatever it might or might not bring turns out to be good or better. Each ending and beginning later generated its own impasse into the 2020s, a stretched-out period of time marked by endless "pre-mediation" (Grusin, 2010) about what the event of Brexit or Trump's (re)election might bring and how, if ever, it might end or, finally, this time, be seized and the US or the UK transformed.

The affective and material legacies of both events continue to reverberate through a formal political scene that feels unusually event-full post 2015, adding to the sense that *this* conjunctural crisis happens as an extended impasse. An impasse full of events but events that very quickly slip from public consciousness, to be replaced by other events that intensely hold attention, before themselves being quickly replaced. Prologuing parliament, sex and financial scandals affecting a serving president, expelling 21 longstanding members of a political party, resignations of multiple prime ministers, "Partygate", incitements to insurrection, insurrections, all appear to matter intensely in the moment and quickly disappear as they blur into one another. Turbulence appears to be the norm, amplified and extended by the interregnum of COVID-19. Past, present, and future blur. "Get Brexit Done", the Conservative Party's slogan at the 2019 election, promised resolution, but as we write in mid-2024, Britain is led by its fourth prime minister since the moment of this resolution. Trump's electoral defeat by Joe Biden in 2020 was swiftly followed by not only the event of the capital insurrection but also the daily premediation of a Trump run for republican nominee. There is no escaping the impasse, resolving the crisis. At least not yet. Even Labour's 2024 general election landslide victory was greeted with claims that the landslide was shallow, perhaps not a victory at all, really.

In conversation with Doreen Massey, Stuart Hall (2010) described what makes a 'conjunctural crisis'. Emphasising the need to address the 'complexity of the crisis as a whole' he stresses a conjunctural crisis involves the coming together, the *fusing*, of disparate elements:

Different levels of society, the economy, politics, ideology, common sense, etc, come together or "fuse". Otherwise, you could get an unresolved ideological crisis which doesn't have immediate political connotations, or which you can't see as being directly related to a change in the economy. The definition of a conjunctural crisis is when these "relatively autonomous" sites – which have different origins, are driven by different contradictions, and develop according to their own temporalities – are nevertheless "convened" or condensed in the same moment. Then there is a crisis, a break, a "ruptural fusion". (Stuart Hall in Hall and Massey (2010): 59–60)

A conjunctural crisis is not a seamless, undifferentiated totality, whereby different 'sites' align and neatly add up without difference or excess. Rather, sites that are ordinarily held in relation but remain different are 'condensed' for a limited open-ended duration (the 'same moment'). *Convened* and *condensed* imply a bringing and holding together, as well as a qualitative shift in the intensity of crises as an effect of the action of condensing or convening.

A conjunctural crisis is therefore characterised by its *density*; it appears to be happening across multiple separate sites at the same time. Crisis in the realm of formal politics, for example, emerges and blurs with crises in the social. A key part of the 'ruptural unity' of this conjunctural crisis has been the articulation of new or reworked social differences and antagonisms as part of the turbulence of the present – around, for example, rural and urban differences, or differences in educational attainment, or through the politics of race amid the anger and dreams of Black Lives Matter and backlashes that desperately reassert a white masculinity that takes new digitally mediated forms, or around generational differences, or gender identity and sexual difference, or the politics of femininity and masculinity after #MeToo, or …

Our ellipsis holds open this conjunctural crisis as unfinished. Above, we have highlighted the most immediately public site of this conjunctural crisis – the turbulence of formal politics since 2008. A key part of the ruptural unity of this crisis are changes at the levels of ideology and common sense, as they fuse and blur with crises in the site of formal politics. A conjunctural crisis happens as the allure or grip of ideas loosens, the horizon of the possible shifts, and that which had been lived as common sense becomes subject to dissensus and dissent again, as questions begin to be felt and alternatives begin to surface.

In the post 2008 period, key to the unsettling of present and future has been the cracking of the ideational-atmospheric complex given the name "there is no alternative", after the phrase forever associated with Margaret Thatcher. "There is no alternative" describes a dispersed structure of feeling through which alternatives to the neoliberal organisation of politics and the economy are mediated and encountered. It legitimises present arrangements through the pre-emptive dismissal of alternatives on the basis of their supposed lack of "realism" – where realism is a felt, habitual judgement that registers how possible an alternative is felt to be (Fisher, 2009). An alternative might be desirable, it might even be the best possible option, but it is felt and dismissed as unrealistic. "There is no alternative" organises the collective horizon of what is felt as possible.

In the conjunctural crisis, "there is no alternative" frays, unravels, ends. Central to this uncertainty about what is ending and what might be beginning is the waning of the "promissory legitimacy" of neoliberalism. Here we extend Beckert's (2020) thesis about the "exhaustion" of the future orientated claims that neoliberalism offered. These were central to the resolution through the 1980s of the conjunctural crisis of the Fordist-Keynesian settlement. Such promises may linger, for example of "growth" or of better futures through becoming an investor in oneself, but, Beckert argues, they lose credibility, the power to motivate action, and the capacity to legitimate. For us, it is less that promises are exhausted and completely detached from, and more that they become fragile, a little harder to attach to, to believe in.

An example is of the promises that gather around neoliberal processes of competitive individualism, the linked figures of the consumer, investor, and entrepreneur, and the principle of meritocracy (Littler, 2018). All of these face a crisis of legitimacy as stories abound of their failure and betrayal. The result is a series of paradoxes that perform the sense of the present as an impasse. The costs of individualism are matters of public concern, around loneliness as governmental object, for example, amid a wider concern with a crisis of intimacy and recognition. New forms of collective life and identification are emerging both on the left and right, in part as digital mediation allows for the fast circulation of affects and formation of new affective communities, not least around fandom. But these detachments from individualism's promises happen alongside an intensified attachment to competitive individualism, refracted through and amplified by whiteness and online forms of masculinity, and enabled by the digital infrastructures and choice architectures that enable life today. We think of figures like Andrew Tate, Elon Musk, or Jordan Peterson, for example. At the same time, new forms of individualism are rehabilitated as injunctions – be passionate (Hong, 2022), be productive (Gregg, 2018), be aspirational (Feher, 2018), be more confident (Orgad and Gill, 2022), and so on – that hold out the promise of being able to get by and flourish after good life fantasies have lost some of their grip, and meritocracy its credibility.

We don't want to overplay the change. Neoliberal promises still hold allure, and we need to know more about the unequal reach of that allure and how it is incited and maintained by capitalism's libidinal economies; of the feeling of freedom through engagement as consumer or investor in the market, of individualised forms of life as mediated through the intensities of digital capitalism, for example. Our point is rather to emphasise an unsettling of neoliberalism's promises, and with them the collective atmosphere given the name "there is no alternative". "Growth" still just about holds out a promise, although of quite what now is unclear, but it is shadowed by the spectre of wealth inequality and ecological crisis and collapse, for example. Neoliberalism's promises are stumbling, confused, just about clinging onto life.

Progressivism, liberalism, and populism are all part of this conjunctural crisis. They have taken their present forms as neoliberal hegemony begins to break down. Later we will identify a set of tendencies that compose the affective present of this conjunctural crisis, but, first, we argue that each political form enacts and reproduces this crisis by operating affectively in the present as an unfolding, available structure of feeling.

Between Affect and Ideology: Structures of Feeling

In the slow crisis of collapsing promises, political antagonism stirs the air. There is a provocation, a call, or a demand for political feeling, for choosing sides. Populism and progressivism magnetise political fields with their intensities; even liberalism, in its defensive crouch, starts to overheat. In the arena of political passions, righteousness and sentimentality mount the podium. Despair and hope commingle, experiment with action. Outrage and contempt project their force fields, creating bubbles of solidarity and exclusion. On the edges and in the middle, there is disaffection, boredom, and confusion. How does one become "sucked in" or "swept up" in these roiling intensities? How do some people (and not others) become attached, for example, to populism's political promise, to progressivism's critique of the present, or to liberalism's story about the (or its own) past?

When we ask what attaches or orients people to populist, progressive, or liberal formations, we might appear to be asking the same longstanding question of "ideology" or even "civic culture" that has percolated through Western political thought since the mid-20th century. But, in fact, both our object of analysis (that which is to be explained) and the mode of our explanation sits askew to these traditions of scholarship. To begin with, although the term "ideology" itself admits multiple uses, neither populism nor progressivism is coherent or codified enough to be considered a "system of ideas" in the ballpark of ideology studies. Populism, with its capacity to appear on the left and the right, has been judged at best a 'thin centred' ideology, with two or three core characteristics (Mudde and Kaltwasser, 2017). More commonly, populism is understood to be a *style* of political rhetoric and performance rather than a political platform (e.g. Norris and Inglehart, 2019; Moffitt, 2016; Block and Negrine, 2017). Progressivism likewise can be attached to multiple political projects, expressing an orientation rather than a coherent system of ideas (Freeden, 2014).

Even liberalism seems to have entered a new "post-ideological" phase. Historically, liberalism presented a coherent and institutionalised system of ideas and values that at times has ascended to hegemonic common sense in the West. Indeed, when Western political theorists declared "the end of ideology" in the mid-20th century, and again in the 1990s, what was left in the wake of great "ideological illusions" of the previous century appeared to be a victorious liberal common sense (Bell, 1962; Fukuyama, 1992). But as liberalism's partiality and pretences have become increasingly more visible, its veneer of inevitability has tarnished, and its claim to universal "common sense" has become less convincing. Entering the contemporary fray alongside populism and progressivism, liberalism too becomes something both less and more than "ideology" in any classical sense.

Introduction

This is not to say that we have no use for the key concepts and questions of ideology critique in the sense that developed from Marxist thought in the late 20th century. Attention to people's attachment to the conditions of their lives, the premise that ideas and feelings have a material basis, and the idea that "common sense" hegemonies are actively stitched together for the exercise of power: these remain critical insights that we pick up in our analysis of our current conjuncture. But at the same time, the historical conditions that we face today present new challenges. What might once have appeared as ideological consistencies are fraying. Both progressive social values and Trump's authoritarian populism are scoring new lines of division while also giving rise to new alliances. An example of such strange cuts and connections is how anti-vaccine positions arose in both populist and progressive camps during the COVID-19 pandemic-period (a convergence, in Naomi Klein's [2023] words, of the 'far right' and the 'far out'). Further (and unlike Thatcherism in its heyday), neither populism nor progressivism have ascended to the role of "common sense" in the Gramscian sense of ideological hegemony. Instead, these political formations are constantly shifting, often gaining momentum as they *veer away* from yesterday's common sense onto the terrain of the more radical, the more "incredible" (e.g. the extremity and undeniably "fringe" aesthetics of the insurrection at the US capitol on 6 January 2021). And while there might be local "hegemonies", such as a set of attitudes and values that define a particular industry (e.g. technology, media, higher education), these localised common *senses* are unable to lay claim to being the *dominant* ideas of a society or an age. We are far from the certainty of "there is no alternative".

In response to our current geohistorical conjuncture and the challenges to living that it poses, we ask again, what is it that assembles in a political formation such as right-wing populism, progressivism, or today's liberalism? How do people become swept up or sucked in, repelled, or dropped out of these loosely knit political consistencies? If ideology is exhausted – that is, if it is 'no longer encompassing', if it 'no longer defines the global mode of functioning of power' (Massumi, 2002: 42) – then what might come after? Our project experiments with Lauren Berlant's (2011: 53) oft-quoted proposition that 'affect theory is another phase in the history of ideology theory' but not in the sense of a linear succession. Instead, we take Berlant's statement as an invitation to be drawn anew – that is, with new vocabularies and conceptual tools – into 'the encounter of what is sensed with what is known' that also was arguably at the heart of ideology critique (Berlant, 2011: 52). *The Politics of Feeling* is an argument for considering how contemporary political forms (of populism, progressivism, and liberalism) take shape under conditions of neoliberal crisis *in the blur* between affect and ideology, the fuzzy zone of their indistinction.

When we refer to populism, progressivism, and liberalism not as alternative ideologies but as *political feelings*, we signal our engagement with Raymond Williams' well-known but endlessly enigmatic concept of 'structures of feeling'.[2] The importance of this concept for us is how it opens onto a space between affect and ideology (Secor and Anderson, 2024). Structures of feeling are political forms (such as populism or progressivism) that are at once recognisable orientations and at the same time *in process*, shifting and unsettled. In *Marxism*

---

[2] Here we learn from how the concept has been taken up in affect related work, in particular the question of the form that collective feeling takes, albeit noting that it has always been slightly askew to the Deleuzian tendencies in affect related work (Berlant, 2011; Closs-Stephens 2022; Highmore, 2017; McCormack, 2023; Anderson, 2014; Coleman, 2018).

and Literature (1977), Williams opens his chapter on structures of feeling with a critique of how cultural analysis tends to take as its object 'formed wholes rather than forming and formative processes' (p. 128). This 'slide towards the past tense and fixed form', Williams argues, is reductive and deadening, overriding the tensions and complexities of lived experience (p. 129). Ideological systems only appear as such belatedly, after certain regularities have been precipitated out of the contemporaneous experience, a principle distilled out of the intensities of feeling of the present. By way of an example Williams points out how the early Victorian *ideological* equation of poverty to social failure was precipitated and generalised from lived *experiences* of fear and shame. This dynamic between the immediate and the formed is at the heart of the concept of structures of feeling. In Williams' own words:

The term [structures of feeling] is difficult, but "feeling" is chosen to emphasize a distinction from more normal concepts of "world-view" or "ideology". It is not only that we must go beyond formally held and systematic beliefs, though of course we have always to include them. It is that we are concerned with meaning and values as they are actively lived and felt, and the relations between these and formal or systematic beliefs are in practice variable [...] We are talking about characteristic elements of impulse, restraint, and tone; specifically affective elements of consciousness and relationships: not feelings against thought, but thought as felt and feeling as thought: practical consciousness of a present kind, in a living and interrelated continuity. We are then defining these elements as a structure: as a set, with specific internal relations, at once interlocking and in tension. Yet we are also defining a social experience which is still in process ... (Williams, 1977: 132).

For Williams, the 'living processes' and 'affective elements' of the social present express certain consistencies or patterns ('structures') that have not already happened but are actively forming in the present. Concerned with how meaning and value are 'actively lived and felt', Williams presents structures of feeling as the *developing form of ideology*, its emergent edge. Even what might gain the marginal coherence of a structure of feeling does not form a singular totality. These are loose weaves, zones where a degree of consistency happens, enough to be recognised and even named (to become 'semantically available' in Williams' terms). Populism, progressivism, and liberalism today linger at the edges of coherence and semantic capture (Anderson, 2014).

When we name populism, progressivism, and liberalism as structures of feeling, we call upon the concept to traverse what might be "in the air" during the conjunctural crisis (fluctuations of affection and disaffection, attachment, and detachment) and what is perhaps difficult to "pin down" but nonetheless *traceable* in the residue of what has already happened (for example, what might be called a "liberal attitude" or a "populist rally"). Ben Highmore, in his book *Cultural Feelings* (2017), shows that Williams at times refers to feelings that are indefinite and diffuse, such as 'feelings of possibility' towards the city (*The Country and the City*, 1973), while elsewhere suggests that structures of feeling correspond to explicit sociopolitical forms (such as the working-class 'democratic feeling' that Williams identified as, 'a crucial aspect of a progressive cultural politics' (Highmore, 2017: 34). In this sense, structures of feeling, while emergent, are also bound up with what Williams would call "residual" forms, those that have already become generalised or distilled.

This understanding of structures of feeling as having the capacity to slide across different states, from the incipient and amorphous to the already passing and specific (in Williams' terms, from the pre-emergent and emergent to the residual and possibly even dominant) takes the concept beyond its appearance in *Marxism and Literature* and is important for our analysis of the politics of feelings. For indeed we find ourselves picking through circulated scenes and events now behind us, even as we unfurl their significance in the present tense and attempt to grasp the import of what inheres in these traces but has not yet been expressed or come fully into consciousness. The analysis that we undertake tinkers at this edge between what has already acquired some kind of regularity (for example, populist passion, progressive moral outrage, or liberal sentiment) and what is still taking shape, where shifts in tone and atmosphere signal the emergence of 'new meanings and values, new practices' and the possibility of change (Williams, 1977: 123).

In the Folds of Structures of Feeling: Difference

As we take the notion of structures of feeling into the political present, we also transform it with relation to the material conditions and concerns of our day. The most significant way that we do this is by activating questions of difference at the heart of the politics of feelings. In *Culture and Society, 1780–1950*, in one of his first uses of the term, Williams tied structures of feeling to distinct generations (Williams, 1958: 119). By the end of his entry on structures of feeling in *Marxism and Literature*, Williams signals 'the complex relation of differentiated structures of feeling to differentiated classes' (Williams, 1977: 134). In a sense, we begin here, where Williams wraps up, but with a perspective on difference that includes class but does not stop there. There are three main ways that we bring questions of difference to the fore in our analysis of the politics of feeling: (1) by emphasising the multiplicity of structures of feeling, (2) by exploring their unevenness and holes, and (3) by examining how they not only operate differentially but actively *produce* difference and relations of domination.

Who gets caught up in political feelings, who is enflamed, and who is alienated, is conditioned by circumstances, orientations, and lived identities. Political scientists and pollsters might pose the question, "Who are the populists?" or "Who are the progressives?" (e.g. Akkerman et al., 2014). Variables such as gender, race, age, class, geographical location, and even "levels of rage" can be factored into complex models to explain differences in attitudes commonly associated with populism, progressivism, or liberalism. Such survey research can evidence significant demographic differences across political "typologies" (e.g. Pew, 2021; 2021b). However, this approach to understanding political phenomena is constrained by its reliance on predetermined categories and a pre-structured political field.

As cultural geographers, our approach to difference and political feeling takes a different tack. For us, the differentiation of allure (e.g. how Farage's visceral performance of frustration and annoyance attracts some and not others) is not just that which is to be explained, but *part of the process* of how, for example, populism becomes *populism in its time and in its place*. That is, populism (or progressivism or liberalism) emerges through the differential availability of populist feelings (or progressive or liberal feelings). The politics of feeling concerns the circulation of collective feelings. But even if these feelings are collective, the capacity to share in a particular moment or scene is differentiated across and within societies. The idea that there are *multiple* structures of feeling in the present, rather than *a* structure of feeling characterising an era, thus provides leverage to open the concept to difference.

This multiplicity also holds out the possibility for 'minor projects of collective world-making' amid those that seem to gather the force of a zeitgeist (McCormack, 2023: 73). Even what might appear to form a localised, dominant consistency (for example, "the progressive university") is not a closed totality or fixed form. Instead, such formations are uneven and full of gaps. Points of dissent, disaffection, or cynicism coexist with (may even be crucial to) the atmosphere of collective feeling. Intensification is accompanied by boredom, attraction by repulsion, sanction by "doubling down". This undulation is not only at work in the *polarisation* of political feelings (for example, when high-voltage accusations of conspiracy or of racism are met with cool indifference) but also *within* what otherwise appears consistent. Recognising the constitutive role of gaps or inconsistencies in the unfolding of collective feeling recalls Slavoj Zizek's insight that the gap between knowledge and belief (encapsulated in the construction, "I know, but nevertheless ...") determines one's 'everyday ideological attitude' (Zizek, 2002: 243). Forming around their own aporetic points, structures of feeling are not only multiple but also "holey": beholden to that which has dropped out or disappeared from their unfolding fabric.

Not only does difference mediate and organise collective feeling, but the reverse is also true. Structures of feeling are not only shaped by difference, but they *produce* difference, they *differentiate*. As political formations, they distribute capacities for certain feelings, orientations, and dispositions across different subjects, sites, and scenes. For example, consider this: in 2020–2021, who had the capacity to be angry at governments about lockdown? And who, on the other hand, was able to be angry at individuals who chose not to mask or become vaccinated? While it may be unsurprising that populist anti-elitism finds expression in pandemic and vaccine scepticism, it is not a given that progressives and liberals would favour regimes of obedience or be more concerned than others for their own health. Feelings such as chafing at government regulation or fearing a novel virus, feelings that one could theoretically imagine being available to anyone (if differently), instead emerged in these times as collective and political. Visceral reactions were conditioned, in the real time of their unfolding, by broader patterns and associations that they also participated in creating. One could say that the patterned distribution of these feelings did not just *reflect* pre-established differences in society but worked *to differentiate* the socio-political-affective present.

In the process of collectivising, structures of feeling are always also creating difference: distributing (in)capacities, affirming certain feelings, dropping others out. There is always the possibility that a gap will open between how one is supposed to feel within a collective and how one is actually affected. This gap produces what Sara Ahmed calls the 'affect alien', the subject who is estranged within a dominant structure of feeling or ideology (such as the 'feminist killjoy' who does not laugh at misogyny) (Ahmed, 2010). If we understand this potential for alienation as internal to structures of feeling, we can recognise that the politics of feeling does not unfold only in a major key. The bluster of the Trumpist sign, 'Fuck Your Feelings', or the high anxiety of the *Atlantic*'s Jan./Feb. 2024 Issue, 'If Trump Wins', do not strike sustained notes without modulation. These feeling-stances do not persist without change or fluctuation. They are always also generating difference, proliferating offshoots, reversing, and collapsing.

In the charged field of a forceful politics of feeling, there are always also "minor feelings" that are at once "out of sync" and *part of what is happening*, part of what matters (Ngai, 2005; Manning, 2016; Hong, 2020). As an example of how "minor feelings" matter, consider pro-Palestinian feeling. Feeling for Palestine and Palestinians (feelings that are not monochromatic but include shades of anger, grief, and righteousness) are *minoritarian* in that they push the limits of sanctioned collective enunciation. Such feelings mounted and became critically important to domestic politics within the US and the UK in the context of Israel's relentless attack on Gaza following the 7 October 2023 Hamas attack. We can discern in this how minor feelings do not just "fall out" of dominant structures but rather unfold a potential for qualitative change in the "common sense" of political feeling.

The complement to attending to the minor is to shine a spotlight on the major: that is, on how structures of feeling both reflect and produce power and subjugation. This leads us to examine the elevation of *white* feeling in populist, progressive, and liberal structures of feeling. We take our cue from work such as Cheryl Matias' book, *Feeling White* (2016), which underscores the ideological role of white emotions in protecting and renewing white racial advantage. Starting from the example of a white woman whose crying in class diverts a discussion of slavery, Matias (2016: 526) critiques 'the racial processes that [...] render Whites' behaviors, emotionalities, discourse, and ideologies as supreme, while socially denigrating the emotionalities of people of Color.' At the same time, it is noteworthy how tears – and the critique of tears, or emotionality more generally – are entangled not only with racialised power but also intersect with gendered and class-based relations of power across different socio-political contexts. For example, right-wing populism is well known to overtly amplify white masculinist grievance (expressed through pumping fists, rather than soulful tears), while performances of progressive white femininity or elite liberal masculinity take different shapes but are equally important to the emotional undercurrents of dominance.

In short, political feelings are feelings of and about power but also feelings *as* power. The concept of structures of feeling helps us tap into consistencies or patterns in how feelings are "gathered up" and become political. As emergent structures of feeling in the blur between affect and ideology, populism, progressivism, and liberalism elevate a "common sense" of feeling, even if this coherence lasts only for a moment, among a certain set of subjects. Alongside the force that catches certain subjects up in an unfolding feeling, there is also always the possibility of alienation, refusal, or reversal. The differentiation occurs not only across variously available political formations but also within and as an inherent part of what happens in their evolving present. Populism, progressivism, and liberalism do not just unfold different modes of political feeling that succeed in attracting different people; they distribute the (in)capacity to feel, to make others feel in certain ways, or to stand aloof from others' feelings. Affective differentiation is how structures of feeling unfold. There is therefore always at once a politics of feeling and a politics of 'feeling otherwise' (to use Yao's term, 2021) in the active present.

Affective Presents

In performing affective differentiation, the three political forms are part of the politics of intensity that has been so central to the sense of a post 2008 conjunctural crisis. They emerge in the wake of the ambiguity that now surrounds neoliberal promises, and respond to and perform the fracturing of 'disaffected' (Gilbert, 2015) and other forms of neoliberal consent. However, the 'affective present' (Berlant, 2011: 4) they are part of is more complex, irreducible to a politics of intensity, and overdetermined by forces that exceed neoliberal logics, forms, and ideals and their (potential) end. There is not a single name that we could easily invoke to describe this present. Despite this, various attempts have been made to diagnose a master key that would unlock the secret to the turbulence of the 15 years since the 2008 financial crisis, some of them recalling past attempts to characterise the West during times in which settlements unsettle; "age of polarisation", "age of uncertainty", "age of insecurity", "age of fear", "age of anger", and so on. While all such attempts disclose something of the present, there main effect is to write out the uncertainty that inevitably follows from trying to diagnose the present as a field of multiple forces. How, then, to characterise the affective present (or better, *presents*) of this conjunctural crisis? And how to do so in a way that avoids writing out difference?

As has been hinted, our method for characterising and sensing the present is to perform conjunctural analysis as a type of diagnostic critique (see Anderson, 2021). As per so much of the recent interest in conjunctural analysis, throughout *The Politics of Feeling* we take inspiration from Stuart Hall and colleagues' analysis of what can retrospectively be seen as material-affective conditions for authoritarian populism in *Policing the Crisis* (Hall et al., 2013) and Hall's attempt to face the troubling appeal of Thatcherism amid a crisis of the left (Hall, 2017).[3] Our reframing of political forms as structures of feeling in part responds to a similar problematic to what

---

[3] For a fuller elaboration of our position on conjunctural analysis see Anderson (2021). As with all recent work on conjunctural analysis, we share the desire to distinguish conjunctural analysis from a straightforward contextualism, stress the multiplicity of different forces that are gathered together through the contingent articulations that (re/de)compose conjunctures, and pay attention to complex forms of causality. Like the work in cultural studies most directly influenced by Hall (e.g. Gilbert 2019; Grossberg 2019; Clarke 2023), and leaving aside the distinctions between Gramscian and Althusserian influences (see Hart, 2024), we emphasise that the practice of tracing articulations is always a situated intervention into the politics of the present (contra the distinction between 'normative' and 'rational' kinds of conjunctural analysis offered by Davidson and Ward (2024)).

Hall set out in *The Great Moving Right Show*: to understand the grounds for the affective appeal of political forms without resorting to any form of crude determinism (or the equally comforting trope of manipulation). Near the conclusion of *The Great Moving Right Show*, Hall reminds his readers of what is really the starting point of his approach:

> But now it must be added [to the understanding of how the new right neutralises the contradiction between the people and the state/power bloc] that this is no rhetorical device or trick, for this populism is operating on genuine contradictions, and it has a rational and material core. Its success and efficacy does not lie in its capacity to dupe unsuspecting folk but in the way it addresses real problems, real and lived experiences, real contradictions—and yet is able to represent them within a logic of discourse which pulls them systematically into line with the policies and class strategies of the Right. (Hall, 2017 [1979]: 185–186)

We agree, as long as the definition of 'rational and material core' and the 'real' can be expanded to include the elements of the affective. Beyond this warning against comforting analysis, we learn from Hall, and collaborators such as Clarke (2023), the necessity of tracing the contingent articulations between the different, inter/dis-connected spatio-temporalities that condition and compose the present's feel and character. For us, and as the discussion of structures of feeling makes clear, it also involves considering structures of feeling and other affective conditions as formed through and formative of conjunctures. Or, to put it simply and in Hall's terms, structures of feeling are part of the 'complex field of power and consent' that conjunctural analysis diagnoses (Hall, in Hall and Massey 2010: 65).

Beginning from the emphasis on difference that all forms of conjunctural analysis share, our aim is not to fix the present under a single name, but to hold steady, for a moment, some of its dominant tendencies. Below we introduce three tendencies that right-wing populism, progressivism, and liberalism are imbricated with.[4] While not exhaustive, and we will refer to other tendencies in the chapters that follow, they provide something of the affective context that the three forms respond to and, in different ways, rearticulate and (re)mediate. Each tendency is at once economic, political, social, and cultural, undermining any analytic separation of them into distinct "levels", "factors", or "domains".[5] In various combinations, they form the affective conditions through which people encounter and attach to the three political forms that have come to inhabit and partially create the present impasse. They are not an 'inert background', or static context (Hall et al., 2013: xiv). Rather, as tendencies that are themselves made up of multiple elements, they connect and disconnect, attach, and detach, in all kinds of ways with other practices, events, and forces to

---

[4] Our use of the term *tendency* is designed to imply collective forces that have a particular direction, have specific geo-historically specific limits and possibilities, affect things outside of themselves, but also are (re)mediated in all kinds of ways as they are articulated with other tendencies, political forms, and events. In gesturing towards real conditions of emergence, the term has resonances with Hall's (2017 [1979]: 179) use of 'precipitating conditions' in his analysis of the emergence of the New Right.

[5] Here we are noting the use of various terms – we could add, as per above, "site" to "level", "factor", or "domain" – that do the work of both highlighting that different kinds of things are drawn together, while also distinguishing between those types of things (see Hart [2024] on how these terms relate to the Althusserian or Gramscian routes of conjunctural analysis).

give this conjunctural crisis its distinctive affective character. And they are all articulated with the slow loss of neoliberalism's promissory legitimacy and the waning of the sense that "there is no alternative" that marks the end of neoliberalism's hegemony.

A Spreading and Intensifying Precariousness?

Everything feels precarious. Well perhaps not everything for everyone everywhere, but at the heart of this conjunctural crisis is a feeling of unwelcome impermanence and perpetual change that the term "precarity" has done so much to orientate attention to since first being popularised in the context of European Mayday protests in the early 2000s. Anna Tsing's (2015: 2) sparse, capacious definition of precarity, 'life without the promise of stability', evokes what, for us, characterises the structure and experience of precarity. Precarity is an economic-political condition, atmosphere, and way of life that happens in the wake of the slow and fast unravelling of a promise: that a stable, predictable life was achievable with something at the subject's disposal (e.g. hard work, the correct attitude, good choices, being white, a specific class position, attaching to a nation).[6]

Populism, progressivism, and liberalism all enact and (re) mediate precarity. Their promises and affective lures are inseparable from problems of living in the midst of 'life without the

---

[6] Here, our emphasis is on precarity in the Global North, in contexts where a nostalgia for the stability of the post-War settlement endures, albeit unevenly. For work on different forms of precarity in the context of the Global South and the logics of ongoing expulsion and dispossession see, for example, Hillenbrand (2023).

promise of stability.' 'Without stability' is, though, not quite right, because promises rarely disappear, and people strive to create handrails within the precarious present, including all kinds of provisional stability and security. But even if the promise just about remains, it becomes ever harder to achieve, a matter of intense, creative, exhausting effort that comes to dominant the present. Perhaps for some the promise wanes. Others cling on, desperately guarding their status against felt threats, others try to remake it as attachments to stable work or home ownership intensify, even as their conditions of realisation become ever more 'problematic' (Berlant, 2011).[7]

When Berlant (2011: 192) claims that precarity is 'the dominant structure and experience of the present moment, cutting across class and localities', they gesture towards this sense of precarity as something more than a labour condition or a socioeconomic category. Not the *sole* structure and experience in the present moment, but "dominant" in the sense of the dominant Williams (1977) works with. Precariousness spreads to those who would appear to have been born into predictable, secure worlds. We can consider, for example, the intensification of anxieties about middle-class status reproduction in the Global North as an example of precarity "spreading" and "cutting across" class locations. The politics of precarity here would be a form of 'elite disappointment', as Eli Thorkelson (2016) puts it, based on fear of losing a secure place in the world as expectations and aspirations for one's own or loved one's lives are placed in question. Likewise, the security offered by

---

[7] This paragraph summarises a large body of work on the resourcefulness of precarious lives, and the difficult work of holding onto promises as their conditions of realisation change (e.g. Taylor, 2024; Silva, 2013; Wilson and Yochim, 2017).

whiteness and certain kinds of hegemonic masculinity are increasingly felt as newly under threat, generating vengeful backlashes against minoritised groups presumed to steal status, security, and enjoyment. Governmental or explanatory categories such as the "squeezed middle", the "just getting by", or the "left behind" are all also symptoms of this spreading precariousness.[8]

Partly, precarity as structure and condition is a consequence of a series of well documented changes to worlds of work in the global north over the past forty years, including the growth of precarious forms of casual, insecure and low wage employment, the reduction of benefits and state protection as the Fordist settlement was dismantled from the late 1970s, and the intensification of conditionality across both wages and benefits. As Isabell Lorey (2015) has argued, the insecurity of precaritisation has become the normal condition of work today, albeit varying in form to include everything from the global managerial class, through the "self-precaritisation" of creative workers and the "algorithmic precaritisation" of gig economy platform workers, to the global underclass of the excluded and immiserated (Hillenbrand, 2023).

Some forms of precarious work might be desired by some subjects,[9] and we need to avoid romanticising post-World War

---

[8] We treat these terms as at once symptomatic of a sense that something is changing at the juncture where shifting post-Fordist class composition meets precaritisation and precariousness, and part of ways of dampening the excess of recent events by providing comforting explanations. They are also all ways in which specific collective subjects are aligned with the affective appeals of different political forms.

[9] On the desire for and attachment to precarious work felt as exciting and offering freedom see Cockayne's (2016) work on the entrepreneurial subject of technology.

II Fordist–Keynesian worlds of stable work and erasing their affective and material injuries. Notwithstanding these differences and caveats, what is shared is the absence of a predictable relation between the here and now and the capacity to make and sustain a good future. Instead, job-based insecurity is what different workers hold in common, albeit a commonality that undermines commonality. Insecurity and individualism fracture shared belonging, such that collective life is partly made through forms of negative solidarity and racialised ressentiment towards the intensely precarious (see Wacquant, 2009). As insecure work becomes the norm and is normalised, precariousness in the world of work folds into a becoming fragile of the forms of life that work enables – the capacity to undertake social reproduction activities, find sources of value and worth in work, and to sustain good life fantasies that nevertheless still just about cling on. Lives teeter on the 'edge of falling apart' (Hillenbrand, 2023), fall apart in slow and fast ways, or are overshadowed by the dread of things falling apart.[10]

Precariousness, on this understanding, is produced through logics of 'precaritisation' (Lorey, 2015) that generate differential experiences of insecurity and exposure to inflation, job losses, and through other ways in which large scale economic changes are felt intimately. Of course, what is now called precarity has long been the norm for most classes of workers in most forms of capitalism, so we need to be careful about claims about newness, as well as the nostalgia for Fordism that is such an important, if residual, part of the present (see Neilson and Rossiter, 2008). The Fordist–Keynesian post-World War II settlement of stable work, stable benefits, and the promise of

---

[10] For work on the relation between precarity and the difficult work of social reproduction to hold together lives see Meehan and Strauss (2015).

upward social mobility was a short-term exception to the rule of capitalist insecurity. The actuality and promise of security up to the mid-1970s was accompanied by the wearing out of classed, racialised populations and the rendering of others as disposable (see Schram, 2015). And today, precarity remains unevenly distributed, with experiences of insecurity amplified through intersecting social differences in ways that categories such as 'hyper-precarity' (Lewis et al., 2015), 'cumulative precarity' (Taylor, 2021), or 'compounded precarity' (Langevang et al., 2022) work analytically and politically to draw our attention to.

But precariousness today is not only a matter of everyday worlds of work-life. Present insecurity and future uncertainty are as much affective qualities, distinct atmospheres, through which a range of economic, environmental, and social event-conditions are (re)mediated. Populism, progressivism, and liberalism all enact and (re)mediate precarity as atmosphere. Witness, for one example, the proliferation and normalisation of crisis in the UK and the US. Anything and everything is in crisis: the NHS, infrastructure, migration, housing, freedom, attention spans, the cost of living, inflation, biodiversity, mental health, elderly care, the climate, masculinity, the nation, democracy itself, the American Dream, and so on. Now invoked in everyday life and media with only the weakest of hopes that crisis is temporary and a return to a non-crisis normality is possible, "crisis" gestures towards a sense of living in the perhaps permanent midst of multiple things continuously and indefinitely and simultaneously falling apart.[11] Looming over these and all the other specific crises and amplifying the

---

[11] The emergence of the term 'polycrisis' to name the present is symptomatic of this proliferation of crisis, its extension to any and all dimensions of life, and the need to therefore understand how crises coexist and amplify one another.

sense of "life without the promise of stability", is climate change as the often-disavowed horizon that brings loss in the present or threatens loss to come.[12]

After the Future?

Crisis is present but "the future" is absent. Amid intensified and spreading precariousness, a specific way of relating to the future is fading. Today populism, progressivism, and liberalism all respond to and enact what Franco Berardi (2011) perceptively called the 'slow cancellation of the future'. Berardi coined the phrase to highlight a dissonance between present political and cultural stuckness and a rhetoric of newness. Of course, something will follow the present, but a particular way of relating to the future has lost its dominance in organising thinking about the unfolding of lives and the movement of society. What has been lost is the future as continuous, linear trajectory that brings with it the expectation of substantial improvement. The future as a time of "progressive betterment" is no longer available as an unequivocal promise to be attached to, or an ambient assumption of the times. Faith in the promise of upward

---

[12] Crisis and the everyday, with the latter as the realm of stable, predictable routines and rhythms and the former a time-limited interruption to the everyday, have taken meaning from one another (see Roitman 2013). The normalisation of crisis-talk, and event-conditions like climate change, undermine the crisis-everyday distinction, a distinction that was only ever available for some. A range of recent concepts – crisis ordinariness, slow disaster, slow violence, slow emergencies, and so on – all attempt to offer new vocabularies in the aftermath of the breaking down of the distinction between normal life and exception.

social mobility, or promises such as meritocracy, also wane as part of the same loss. Formations such as the America Dream begin to creak.

Berardi's claim is about a loss of a relation and belief that animated political and cultural modernity, including the Fordist-Keynesian settlement. Key to his diagnosis is the claim about the "slow" pace or rhythm of loss. He details a gradual disintegration of the belief in a future of progressive betterment, much as above we highlighted the ambiguity and ambivalence that now surrounds neoliberal promises, rather than their straightforward end and absence.

The result of this slow cancellation has been a scrambling of the lines between past, present, and future, and the emergence of new temporal forms, the most significant of which we elaborate in the chapters that follow on each political form or "structure of feeling". Whether it be the echoes of lost past futures that Mark Fisher (2014) writes about, or the jolts of dark apocalyptic "misfutures' (Fleming, 2019) that rupture the present, the future is less a path forward, perhaps with some bumps and obstacles along the way, and more a matter of loops where pasts return, blanks beyond which imagination is not possible, or nihilistic visions of literally no future in the midst of the catastrophic imaginaries of extinction that fill the crisis present.

Our starting point that a once dominant relation with the future is being lost requires clarification. For one, we can think of how the 'slow cancellation of the future' coexists with continuing, even sometimes intensifying, forms of 'reproductive futurism' (Edelman, 2004) as the linearity of heteropatriarchal time is held onto. In some ways, this is what Berlant (2011) teaches us: that attachments to stable, knowable futures intensify once the future is newly placed in question, even if their conditions of realisation become ever more problematic.

And it is clear that the belief in the time of progressive betterment was unequally distributed along class and racial lines, despite multiple subjects being in the orbit of promises like the American Dream or post-World War II prosperity; further, it was built on the damage, suffering, and loss of slavery and colonialism, and their ongoing legacies. As work in Black and indigenous studies insists, particularly work in the orbit of afropessimism (Warren, 2018), the future as abyssal catastrophe occasioned by anti-Black violence and the dispossession of indigenous peoples is the material and affective condition for linear, progressive time. Indeed, the presence or not of "the future" has always been and remains productive of differences, with the legacies of the unequal availability of and attachment to "the future" now folding into ways of relating to the future "after progress", including in the slow death of toxic legacies (Ahmann, 2024). Habiba Ibrahim and Badia Ahad (2024: 2) detail, for example, how the prolonged time of overlapping global crises become ordinary are lived through what they call 'black temporalties', constituted through 'a sense of liminality that is neither past or present; instead the time of crisis feels more like flight than arrival'.

To be more specific, then, the gradual disintegration of belief in the future is a problem for many, but particularly so for those white, middle-class subjects who were once in proximity to the cluster of good life fantasies that enacted and reproduced belief in the future. Anxieties about the reproduction of middle-class status is, in part, a problem of the end of an ambient surety about the better future that partly constituted mid-20th century middle classness in both the UK and US. Newspaper or magazine articles that announce, for example, that this generation's economic prospects have diminished and will fall behind their parents for the first time perform the anxiety that follows from the loss of the assurance of the future.

The slow cancellation of the future is, then, not only a loss to be lamented, given the time of the future was only ever available for some, and barely or never present for others. As well as an intense holding on to "the future" and nihilisms that proclaim no future, the end of "the future" opens the possibility of other relations, something we have witnessed in the decade or so since Berardi was writing as the sense that "there is no alternative" has loosened in the long aftermath of the 2008 financial crisis. Perhaps we can understand recent experiments that rehabilitate past futures, or make the present into the past of a future justice yet to come, as the stirrings of a new capacity to imagine otherwise as part of a living tradition of 'freedom dreams' (Kelley, 2002)? Perhaps in the wake of the slow cancellation of "the future" what is emergent or pre-emergent is a fast and slow proliferation of other futures? We hear this stirring across numerous movements from the margins that create forms of 'counter-hegemonic time' (Ibrahim and Ahad 2024: 7): afrofuturisms, queer experiments in living otherwise, the brief life of Acid communism in the UK, parts of the ecological movement, Black Lives Matter, the reclamation of the time of care and rest in feminist and disability activist movements, and so on. Beyond the progressive left, we find a concern with the distant future where the libertarian right meets today's platform capitalism. The far future of human life untethered from Earth replaces the linear time of continuous progress in "long termism" and other Silicon Valley forms of techno-optimism, for example.

A proliferation of other relations with futures is part of what happens at the end of the future. Losing "the future" is an ongoing, multiple process. Other relations with futures multiply, new relations between past–present–future are performed, but "the future" is also desperately, sometimes violently, held onto and promised anew. Populism, progressivism, and liberalism are all responses to the problem of how to relate to and feel the future today amidst its end.

Digitally Mediated Presents?

At the same time as a geo-historically, unevenly available relation with the future is slowly cancelled, the experience of the present changes. Precarity names part of that change, where the present is characterised by uncertainty and insecurity, just getting by absorbs attention and energy, to borrow Berlant's (2011) phrasing, and future threats seem to loom over a here and now in the crisis present. As important as this present is to our three political forms, precarity does not exhaust changes in the spatial-temporal organisation of the "present". Nor do we think a single account is possible. We take seriously, instead, the tensions and contradictions between different diagnostic attempts to grasp and name what is happening to the present as the micro times of everyday life become inserted into the flows and networks of platform capitalism. Has the present been expanded or compressed, disappeared, or become perpetual?

The contradictory feel of the present is inseparable from forms of digital mediation, in the context of the becoming dominant of platform capitalism (see Gilbert and Williams, 2022). It is from within digitally mediated networked 'now time' (Coleman, 2020) that each structure of feeling is felt, encountered and related to. They take form as structures of feeling in part through their digital mediation. Some of the conditions for each of the political forms are evoked in the anxieties that now regularly surface about the negative consequences of digital mediation for the fast circulation of information and images, the creation of value through outrage and other vehement feelings, (in)capacity to attend, the reversals and indistinctions of the private and public, and the creation of affective-ideational bubbles and the proliferation of micro-publics. It is, however, important to avoid accounts that equate the media saturated, networked present with strong stories of a 'lost grip on time, memory and focus alike' (Paasonen, 2020: 12). Rather, we see pessimistic judgments of a flattened and distracted present as indicative of some kind of change that undoubtedly matters to politics today, but, at the same time, we pause before affirming narratives of loss that lament change, repeat the anxieties that always gather around new forms of media, and perform a restorative nostalgia for a rational public that never really existed.

Suspending judgement, what matters for understanding politics in this conjunctural crisis are the multiple species of time that populism, progressivism and liberalism as structures of feeling happen through. One of those times is the intensified present of live "real time", organised around instantaneity and the feel of immersion in the real as it happens. Described by Anna Kornbluh (2024) as 'presence without future' (p. 6, n9) and producing a 'beclouded nonhorizon' (p. 13), immediacy promises the always available intensity of pure, unmediated presence. Immediacy finds affective expression in the movements of outrage through which value is constructed via mockery, hyperbole, and other practices in the bleed between new media and legacy media (Berry and Sobieraj, 2016).

Another temporality stands in contrast to the immersion and intensity of "real-time" immediacy. A key habitual digital practice is simply checking or updating a device or app in a way that creates the anticipation of a possible event in a present now stretched between the here and now and a possible future (Grusin, 2010). Possible breaking news, a funny meme, images of a genocide, a message from a not heard from in a while friend, the present is full of these and other 'mediated micro-events'

(Passonen, 2020: 21) through the form of updates and notifications. The digitally mediated present is stretched out into a near future and the ever-present possibility of something, which might be nothing, happening. Everyday life is made newly full of possibilities, albeit of minor not quite events.

Other habitual digital practices such as scrolling or refreshing streams and feeds, by contrast again, create an elongated, always unfolding present. Often serving as a temporary respite from the digitally mediated sense that time is accelerating or running out, the continuously unfolding present is one in which newness and sameness blur (see Coleman, 2020). The present is at once 'contracted and expanded so that it is, at the same time, new, continuing, and stilled or paused' (Coleman, 2020: 74). The space of the stream or feed is also a space of fragments and juxtapositions. One second a Trump meme, the next an image of an unfolding genocide, and then perhaps a cute cat. As structures of feeling, populism, liberalism, and progressivism are made present across multiple affective scenes.

The digitally mediated present through which political forms are encountered and mediated becomes a matter of intensely mixed feelings, as the intensity of immediacy mixes with the blur of the scroll or anticipation of possible quasi-events. Dullness and excitement coexist, boredom and interest overlap, and outrage and indifference blur. Perhaps mixed feelings are always-already part of everyday life, one lesson of those affect theories most influenced by queer theories, but there seems to be something about digital mediation that intensifies their proximity and makes navigating them into an everyday task. For example, the drift of scrolling is felt by some users as at once an occasion of respite from a too demanding world, boring, momentarily exciting, and a waste of time. In that drift, an extended present is felt and experiences surface that our inherited taxonomies for naming and knowing affective life seem to miss (Chun, 2017). Clear lines between good and bad digital feelings, positive or negative experiences, are hard to achieve. Mixed feelings, and quick oscillation between seemingly opposed affective states that are felt ambivalently, become the affective signature of the digital present.

Each political form is still encountered amid everyday lives that are composed of far more than digital mediation. Nevertheless, it is through the different presents partly produced through the digital that populism, progressivism, and liberalism are encountered as structures of feeling. Scenes, figures, and events that compose each political form become part of a present that might have disappeared, expanded, become endless, or been compressed. What each political form, and its mode of affective presence and appeal and allure, do to the structure and experience of the digitally mediated present is an open question.

Propositions from the Present

Spreading and intensifying precarity, the cancellation of the future, the digitally mediated present; our map of spatio-temporal tendencies is not designed to be exhaustive or to add up to a seamless, integrated whole. Each tendency is multiple. They contain the contradictions and paradoxes that animate socio-cultural life as neoliberal hegemony ends and something new emerges. Our aim has been to diagram some of the tendencies that compose the conjunctural crisis that connects the UK and US, while holding onto some of the differences with which each tendency is articulated. Other tendencies, and other differences, will surface over *The Politics of Feeling*.

Our crisis prone present is uneasily tensed between the end of a settlement and a set of branching, emergent possibilities for what might replace the hegemony of neoliberalism.

Populism, progressivism, and liberalism in their current forms are affective response to the problems of living that people face from within this affective present. If precarity is a common experience, albeit intensely different in experience, how do the different political forms relate to insecurity and uncertainty and the individualism of "life without the promise of stability"? What kind of future can be promised or offered in the aftermath of the slow cancellation of the modernist, future of perpetual progressive betterment? How can the present be inhabited in a way that feels good, after the lines between everyday life and the digital collapse? If each form offers a promise of resolution to these shared problems, they also, in different ways, refract and rearticulate them, offer different accounts of responsibility and blame, and, on occasion, bring them into being. Promises are offered and betrayed.

Written over the course of five years, this is a book about the unfolding present but, as such, it can only be about the past. Bookended by the 2024 UK general election and US presidential election, we have attempted to make some sense of the post 2008 conjunctural crisis while writing from a multiplicity of moments that each generated their own intensity, gathered up the past in a certain way, suggested certain futures, only to be undone in the wake of what happened. A question posed in 2022 about whether Trump's defeat would live on as a "bad omen" for right-wing populism seems naïve from the vantage point of 2024. The writing of any present slips into a record of the past. Now caught up in a new moment, we flag the passage for revision. How can we write into the experience of the present, into all that has not yet revealed its import, not yet been tempered by its own future?

There is no solution to this.

We have no choice but to stay with the trouble of writing the fleeting present into an uncertain future. Throughout this book, moments erupt in their unscripted singularity, only to sink back down into what became of them: their obscurity, their re-interpreted significance, their shifting affective valences. What was once invested with sincere concern becomes funny. What was once funny becomes sickening. What once provoked a flutter of hope becomes a hollow reminder of what has since been lost. The present is a syncopated beat, continuously displaced. This confounding untimeliness is the condition of our attempt to situate our analysis at the developing edge of political feeling. We gather materials for analysis and place them within the colliding currents of our times. The scenes and fragments that we analyse – from eruptions of political eventfulness to antics of politicians, the pronouncements of pundits, or the emotive streams of social media "takes" – are residual, in the sense that Williams used this term. He writes, 'The residual, by definition, has been effectively formed in the past, but it is still active in the cultural process, not only and often not at all as an element of the past, but as an effective element of the present' (Williams, 1977: 122). In other words, it is precisely in their continual re-signification that these elements participate in experiences of the present, in what becomes feelable or sensible in a particular time and place.

Our mode for staying with the always unfinished, always becoming residual, affective present is to offer *propositions*. Each chapter offers three propositions about how one of the political forms operates affectively. Partly our aim in offering propositions is diagnostic. They are answers to the question of how a structure of feeling relates to the tendencies that make up the affective present and offers a specific kind of affective appeal and allure. But we recognise that the propositional mode may appear out of sync with our own framing. After stressing the ambiguity and multiplicity of structures of feeling and the affective present, a series of bold statements might seem to imply certainty, to perform authority and external vantage point, as though whoever proposes the propositions stands apart from and surveys a moving present. Such a propositional style runs counter to more established ways of writing to stay with the ambiguity of affective life (e.g. Berlant and Stewart, 2019; Stewart, 2017). And yet, we conceive of these propositions as another way to respond to ambiguity and emergence. Perhaps counterintuitively, by presenting our analysis in the form of propositions, we attempt to remain open to what is happening in this conjunctural crisis, to move around the problem of political feeling without exhausting it. As claims, our propositions are designed to be generative of a distinctive orientation to some aspect of the moving present, one in which any number of such propositions might be floated, defended, shot down. As a glimmer or a flash of an assertive claim, their capacity to be sunk is as important as whatever insight they momentarily provide.

Propositions are always provisional and contestable, subject to revision and reworking, or indeed rejection, as they are received and responded to. We hope you disagree with some of them. There can also be a playfulness to propositions that undermines the certainty we perform in naming them. We are trying things out with them, in the spirit of Stuart Hall's analysis of the new right. We are moving around problems, attempting to clarify them, temporarily holding some things still to see what we might notice anew about this conjunctural crisis. We offer them as part of the always unfinished, always necessary, political project of conjunctural analysis – to think differently about the unfolding present.

In the first substantive chapter we address right-wing populism, simultaneously a dangerous spectre, an invested promise, and an enjoyed spectacle that has marked the post 2008 political impasse. Indeed, accounts of the post-2008 conjunctural crisis are so often reduced to fascinated and horrified accounts of right-wing populism, its causes, forms, and futures. Our first proposition – *Populism offers affirmation and promises recognition* – intervenes directly into these debates. We argue that right-wing populism holds out the promise of recognition to those who feel they lack present recognition, in particular the subjects of 'dethroned' (Brown, 2019) white masculinity. Affirmation is an important part of this promise but so is absolution – that difficulty, that loss, is the responsibility of something or someone that is not you. Breaking with the neoliberal responsibilisation of the self, right-wing populism affirms resentment both towards specific racialised others, in particular immigrants, but also the "elite" or "establishment" that has enabled others to take or be given more than they deserve. Next, our second proposition – *Populism is excessive* – shifts to the register of populist performances. There we find that populism performs an affective break that re-potentialises the present, creating the fissure of excessive intensity as a counter to disaffection. Finally, and looping back to the cancellation of the future, we argue that the excess of right-wing populism coexists with a "time-loop" optimism, whereby the good not-quite lost past becomes the better future to be returned to after the present is disrupted. Allowing for the reattachment of lost objects, right-wing populism solves (and reenacts) the problem of the absence of the future by finding it waiting in the past: *Populism is optimistic*. Recognition and resentment are the conditions for this time-loop optimism.

Next, we turn to progressivism, so often written out of stories of the present, or the object of intense hatred and mockery as part of the "war on woke". There we find that things are bad and getting worse. The present is a disaster, the future is foreshadowed by catastrophe, but unlike for right-wing populism, the past cannot be recovered. Our first proposition – *For progressivism, while things are not good, they also haven't been better* – marks out this key temporal difference with right-wing populism. There are no good objects in the past unambivalently available to be attached to in the way the past exists for populists, unless in the form of traces of heroic defeat and justice just barely glimpsed. But what is worse than the past, is the future. For in the midst of multi-interlocking crises, the future is related to as a catastrophe unfolding in the present. Progress is no longer available for progressives to attach to. If populism solves the problem of the absence of the future by finding optimism in the past and gathers its intensities where resentment meets time loop optimism, our second proposition is that *Progressivism is intensified by its own impasse*. This impasse, we argue, is not only the gap between the promise of progress and the bad future to come but also a fissure within the progressive structure of feeling that elevates white affect and white political redemption by projecting the destruction that has already been accomplished onto the horizon. Our third proposition – *For progressives, everything matters now* – focuses on how, as a result, everything is at stake in the present moment. For the right action here and now has the capacity to redeem the past and to forestall or end the catastrophe to come. The problem of the absence of the progressive future is solved by a heightened attention to anything and everything in the present.

How does liberalism respond to its own crisis, amid the loss of its felt status as common sense and the intense challenge from both right-wing populism and progressivism? This is the subject of our final substantive chapter. Our first proposition is that liberalism changes tone as it attempts to desperately re-establish its own hegemony, becoming newly defensive and bellicose. Hence, *Liberalism must be defended*! What was once common sense needs to be defended now that the mood of "there is no alternative" has been broken. But there is no going back, and the very act of defence performs the break with common sense that liberalism is desperate to repair. Next, we home in on liberalism's tragic search for good objects that would enable a new love for liberalism, given the difficulties of reestablishing liberalism as common sense. Unfortunately for liberals, none of the potential objects of attachment, whether the Ukraine War or Truth for example, can provide an exit to the impasse by creating a newly intense attachment to liberalism. Consequently, *melancholy, liberalism faces a crisis of attachment*. In our final proposition we propose that liberalism, faced with the absence of objects of attachment, solves its crisis of attachment by offering a particular promise to subjects who desire the non-political: *Liberalism promises nothing ever need change*, including, and perhaps especially, a classed and gendered articulation of white privilege. Liberalism instead offers the weak hope of being able to get on with life again without having to think or feel too much about politics. It offers the promise of exiting the conjunctural crisis by enjoying the muted pleasures of detachment. "Change" is the feeling of the political disappearing.

In our final moments with this manuscript, we are in the immediate aftermath of Trump's second victory in November 2024. The political enjoyment of the day belongs to someone else. We are plunged into a new version of the present in which we sense that the politics of feeling is being reconfigured for another phase. It is too soon to know how this event or others currently unfolding (e.g. ongoing wars, effects of climate change, the cost-of-living crisis, or the next pandemic) will condition and reconfigure political feelings to come. This book cannot endlessly evolve, and so it stops short, sometime in 2024. But we do maintain, and *Politics of Feeling* attempts to demonstrate, that what happens next in the realm of politics will be shaped by the differentially distributed capacity and inclination *to feel* something, to be moved, to be left cold, to connect to what is on offer or to be repelled by it. Who despairs and who grabs a whisp of hope from the air? Who reaches for the political intensity of solidarity or of an angry mob? Who feels threatened or abandoned, and who turns away, shuts down, or gets bored? What happens when a conjunctural crisis fuels the proliferation of alternatives – and this in turn creates ever-greater intensity, ever-greater alienation? What follows is a series of momentary propositions, offered up like logs to grab hold of in the rapids of the politics of feeling.

2
Populism: Affirmative, Excessive, and Optimistic

Introduction: Weak Ideology, Strong Feelings

During his 2016 campaign to become Republican presidential nominee, at a meeting with the editorial writers of *The New York Times* Donald J. Trump talked about applause lines at his rallies: 'You know ... if it gets a little boring, if I see people starting to sort of, maybe thinking about leaving, I can sort of tell the audience, I just say, "We will build the wall!" and they go nuts' (Editorial Board *NYT*, 2016).

For the editorial writers at *The New York Times*, the intentionality of Trump's public performance was evidence of a questionable relation with the audience who 'go nuts'. Invoking the longstanding spectre of the politician who deceptively manipulates the unruly passions of the unwitting masses, they discuss how Trump invents policy and political positions: 'His supporters say they don't care. What they may not know is how deliberately he is currying their favor.'

They may not know, but perhaps they did know. What if someone 'deliberately currying their favor' was felt as a form of care and exactly what was desired? Trump's applause line and the muted critique by *The New York Times* editorial board indicates the complexities of the affective politics of right-wing populism. The conditional '*may* not know' (emphasis added) in the editorial hints to a crisis of response before a form of political performance where bellicose nationalism and racialised resentment gather around the "wall" and mix with collective enthusiasm and the intensity of a violent fun against a background of potential boredom.

Almost ten years on from this scene and in the wake of still more dramatic scenes of incitement and affection, we address right-wing populism in a way that stays with the ambiguities of the (or its) moment. In June 2024, right-wing populist candidates campaigned for office not only in the US and the UK, but also in France, where Marine Le Pen's far right nationalist party suddenly had a chance to take control of the government. Earlier that month, in the EU parliamentary elections, right-wing populist parties had made substantial gains and on 1 July, Hungary's Viktor Orbán took on the rotating six-month presidency under the Trumpian slogan, 'Make Europe Great Again'. Was this the populist moment waxing? Or was it an illusion, a convergence of opportunities and forces that would dissipate by winter? Even as these events slip into "what happened", we write (we cannot but write) in a transitional moment. Something is about to happen. It is not clear what we are living after, let alone what we might be waiting for. We can "update" our text but the uncertainty moves with us, renews itself. Perhaps these repeating "populist moments" – they arise, they pass, they return, do they pass again? – are part of a string of incremental moments in the ongoing "end" of neoliberalism, where the much heralded "crisis" of neoliberalism after the 2008 financial crisis tips over into the advent of even darker illiberalisms?

Put differently, we don't know whether right-wing populism is our past, our present, or our future, or all three simultaneously. From within this uncertainty, we pause to explore the structure of feeling of right-wing populism in the UK and the US. We describe and speculate on how feelings and atmospheres condition how right-wing populisms emerge and take shape. But also, we are trying to grasp how right-wing populism unfolds in the present as a set of possible feelings and orientations that 'exert palpable pressures and set effective limits on experience and on action' (Williams, 1977: 132). How does right-wing populism gather up certain feelings and orientations and how do these feelings in turn give substance to this emergent political formation?

We are far from the first to consider the relation between populism and affect. By advocates and critics alike, collective feelings are frequently invoked as causes of or conditions for the emergence of contemporary right-wing populisms. These stories of unruly passions normally centre strong, dramatic, collective feelings which constitute the white, post-industrial "left behind", principally anger and frustration but also a chaotic mix of broader insecurities about status in times of shrinking hope. Debates have proliferated around *which* collective feelings to centre and what is at stake in these choices. Does, for example, focusing on "economic anxiety" in post-industrial peripheries obscure the significance of racialised anxiety and resentment in fuelling populist feeling? But it is not just that populism takes advantage of existing discontents. Right-wing politicians and campaigns evoke, solicit and produce anger, anxiety, and resentment. It is no surprise or accident that editorial writers of *The New York Times* choose to highlight candidate Trump's affective performance.

There is something comforting about accounts of the emotional roots of populist politics, even as they paint a dark picture of a maelstrom of smouldering resentments and intensifying angers that partly compose the turbulence of the post 2008 financial crisis conjuncture. The overspill, the excess, of populism is enrolled into a narrative which offers the consoling certainties of explanation. Collective affects play a mediating role in these accounts, solving the puzzle of how a set of political-economic transformations find expression in the emergence and success of populist parties and politicians. As with all explanatory work, these accounts help stabilise the phenomena to be explained (Latour, 1988). They also perpetuate some classic political tropes and characters. The public is deceived by a cunning leader; the savvy critic reveals the manipulation. Or the people get a hold of the truth thanks to an iconoclastic leader, and the elite critics attempt to discredit them as deluded and ignorant. The zenith of this genre are accounts that make right-wing populism into a symptom of a broader becoming-affective or emotional of politics, where facts are replaced by affective facts (Massumi, 2015) in a disorientating, dissonant, post-truth era. In short, a kind of "strong theory" of populism in Eve Sedgwick's (2003) sense is enabled that enrols the politics of feeling for the purpose of centring post-industrial dynamics of race and class.

Elements of these stories will surface across our account. Our starting position, beginning from our opening scene, is that the politics of feeling are a little more complicated, with right-wing populism serving as something to be explained and a warning but also as an emergent structure of feeling in and for our times. Right-wing populism has been narrated as uniquely affective or emotional, a quality that makes it both alluring and repelling to opponents. One response by those advocating a "left-wing populism" has been to find in articulations of the people and their passions a route to renewed political engagement (e.g. Frank, 2020; Smith, 2019). For whether a tweet, or a photo-op, a meme or a joke by a late-night comedian, digitally mediated populist performances are very much part of political feeling in the US and the UK today. They gather attention as they are circulated through social media ecologies where economic and other types of value are created through attention and movement, and new articulations of race, class and gender take affective form (for example, see Baspehlivan

(2024) on 'reactionary memescapes'). While scholars continue to argue about whether feelings in themselves matter at all (or are derivative of material conditions), questions of *whose* feelings matter and whose are superfluous, of whose feelings are genuine and warranted and whose are "whipped up", and even of *which* emotions are most appropriate or effective politically continue to rile up public debate. Outrage becomes both the fuel of political action and a pleasurable release in and of itself. Populist scenes have been *enjoyed* as occasions for strong feeling in a digitally mediated world in which lines between flatness and intensity, attention and distraction, engagement and disengagement, are increasingly blurred.

How to relate to this ambivalent field, already full of stories and arguments about feelings? And how to do so during a seeming never-ending production of claims and counter claims about what populism is and how to distinguish between populisms? We offer a set of propositions about right-wing populism, focusing on the US and the UK over the past decade. These two cases sit side by side both familiarly and with some perplexity. In 2016, with Nigel Farage touting a vote to leave the European Union as a 'victory for real people' and Trump promising to transfer power from Washington 'back to you, the American people', there was a growing consensus that a common current had been gathering force in both societies and had broken the dam with the success of these campaigns on either side of the Atlantic (Norris and Inglehart 2019: 18; Farage, 2016; Trump, 2017). As Trump crowed on the eve of his first election victory, 'It'll be Brexit plus plus plus!' – an American, supersized version of what UKIP and Vote Leave had achieved (Mardell, 2016). Capitalising on anti-immigrant sentiment and, in their different ways, promising to "get it done" in opposition to bureaucratic power and entrenched political interests, both Trump and then Boris Johnson appeared to have leveraged their electoral successes via right-wing populism (Bogaards, 2017; Cox 2017; Gusterson, 2017). Yet one might quickly gauge the distance between how right-wing populism's 2016 surge played out across the two societies by comparing Johnson's exit from office (by vote of no confidence in 2022) to Trump's explosive attempt to hang onto power following his loss in the 2020 US national election.

Despite the real cultural and material differences between the two contexts, there remains something to be gained politically and theoretically by taking populism as an analytic for understanding the affective politics of the right-wing in the UK and the US. Partly this is because at the time of writing, in 2024, right-wing populism is once again central to electoral politics in both countries, with resonances between Trump's Republican presidential campaign and both Nigel Farage's Reform Party and parts of the Conservative Party's campaign. But it is also in part because populism remains above all "available" as a way of constructing what Chantal Mouffe (2005) calls "politics" – that is, the division of society into an antagonism between "us" and "them". Populism is not only available to fascistic and white supremacist leaders such as Trump but also to leaders like Boris Johnson who mix renewed nationalism with neoliberal elements; it is available to left-wing movements as well, though such articulations are beyond the scope of our analysis here. Thus while "Trumpism" has come to embody right-wing populism in the US, in the UK different political figures have become invested with populist feeling at different times, demonstrating the mobility and availability of populism, not as a pre-formed category but as an emergent political formation that is continuously being reshaped in the present.

Although populism, in the thinness of its content, can attach to left or right politics, we focus our chapter on "right-wing" (conservative) populism because of its pressing concern in the US and the UK at the present time. This is not to draw an impermeable line between left and right populisms, for indeed the structure of feeling we analyse often seems to sweep up elements typically associated with the left (such as, for example, when Boris Johnson mobilises a vocabulary of justice to legitimise the strategy and promise of "levelling up", or when Trump appeals to those "left-behind" by globalisation). Beyond the UK and the US, this blurring is particularly found in Latin American populisms, which are often animated by anti-imperialist and anti-oligarchical impulses (de Genova, 2018). In Western Europe and North America, left-wing populism may be less overtly present, but it sometimes appears as an idea invested with hope, offering the only effective counter to populisms of the right (e.g. Mouffe, 2018).[1]

By presenting three propositions on *right-wing* populism and speaking narrowly across the US and the UK contexts, our aim is not to pin down populism as a political formation, nor to exhaust all its possibilities, but to trace out certain consistencies of feeling that take their bearings in relation to the conditions present. These conditions include an atmosphere of global right-wing populist power buoyed by the rise of authoritarian populist leaders (in Russia, Hungary, India, Brazil, and Turkey) and the growth of support for right-wing populist parties in Western Europe (e.g. the near-miss of Marine Le Pen's bid for power in France in the summer of 2024). While there are commonalities of tone as well as multiple practical connections across our cases and populisms around the world (for example, overlaps between the Viktor Orbán administration in Hungary and elements in the UK Conservative Party and US Republicans, or between Trump and the former Brazilian

---

[1] For reflections on left-wing mobilisations of 'the people', see Bosworth (2019).

President Jair Bolsonaro's shared reversal of even minimal climate change polices), we would caution against any single claim about the global affective present and right-wing populisms (as in the announcement of a global 'age of anger' [Mishra, 2017]). We offer our propositions as a response to the unfolding dynamics and the politics of feeling in the US and the UK and invite readers to wonder about the commonalities and differences with other populisms.

Beginning from the premise that right-wing populism refers to a complex of experiences, relations, attitudes, and orientations that are continuously taking shape in relation to (and as part of) the troubled conditions of the present, our aim is to provide some insight into right-wing populism as a contemporary structure of feeling in the US and the UK. What sensations, feelings, habits of thought, and conceptions of the world does right-wing populism bundle together? And what does it drop out: what ways of feeling or relating does it incapacitate or delegitimate, and for whom? How might we grasp the active, formative, and transformational processes of right-wing populism while it is ongoingly taking shape in all the moments of our apprehension?

In what follows, we sift through the scenes and moments of our times, pulling on strands of feeling that help us to unravel the fabric of right-wing populism in our times (and places). Our first proposition, *populism offers affirmation and promises recognition*, argues that right-wing populism offers the promise of recognition to the 'dethroned' (Brown, 2019) through the drawing of an "antagonistic front" that necessitates some form of anger or hatred or contempt orientated towards *other* subjects who have taken or been given too much recognition. Our second proposition, *populism is excessive*, addresses the affective fullness of populism by showing how populism promises its subjects access to a *different* feeling (in contrast to the impassive ordinariness of "no alternative") as well as *a feeling of difference* that underscores the fundamental antagonism of populist politics. Finally, building from our emphasis on a particular articulation of recognition and excess, we propose that right-wing populism is a form of optimism that responds to the slow cancellation of the future: *populism is optimistic*. In conclusion, we turn directly to the question of the futures of right-wing populism as a structure of feeling in the midst of its continual end and return.

Proposition 1: Populism Offers Affirmation and Promises Recognition

'You know, to just be grossly generalistic, you could put half of Trump's supporters into what I call the basket of deplorables. Right?', Hilary Clinton unwisely remarked at a fundraiser in New York City during the 2016 presidential campaign. Unsurprisingly, Donald Trump was quick to respond. In a speech a few days later in Baltimore, he attacked Clinton's comments in typical populist style, castigating her elitism, and claiming shock and alarm on behalf of 'wonderful, amazing people':

I was thus deeply shocked and alarmed this Friday to hear my opponent attack, slander, smear, demean these wonderful, amazing people who are supporting our campaign by the millions. Our support comes from every part of America and every walk of life. We have the support of cops and soldiers, carpenters and welders, the young and the old, and millions of working class families who just want a better future and a good job. These were the people Hillary Clinton so viciously demonized.

These were among the countless Americans that Hillary Clinton called deplorable, irredeemable and un-American. Nobody's heard anything like this. She called these patriotic men and women every vile name in the book; she called them racist, sexist, xenophobic, Islamophobic. She called half of our supporters a "basket of deplorable" in both the speech and an interview. She divides people into baskets as though they were objects, not human beings. (Trump quoted by Blake, 2016)

The "basket of deplorables" label was quickly emblazoned across mugs and T-shirts as it became part of the commercial culture of the Trump campaign alongside "Make America Great Again" caps and "Build the Wall" bumper stickers. T-shirts sold on the Trump campaign website turned the phrase into an identity to be attached to, perhaps with humour and irony: 'I am a deplorable.'

Trump's enthusiastic defence of 'wonderful, amazing people', a group who later in the same speech he simply called 'hardworking Americans', was an early example of a recurrent feature of the affective appeal of right-wing populism since 2008: an affirmation of the worth and value of people who could now lay claim to being mis- or un-recognised. Groups who, to use Wendy Brown's (2019) term, felt 'dethroned' from their prior position and status or, to supplement her term, perhaps felt like they had never ascended to pre-eminence, and maybe had not. Clinton's 'basket of deplorables' served to dramatise a liberal lack of recognition and contempt that lurked within the collective sense that "there is no alternative". This frisson of contempt had surfaced in other political scenes and became minor scandals in the period after the 2008 financial crisis. Gordon Brown, for example, was recorded during the 2010 UK general election privately describing a member of the public as 'that bigoted woman' after she had expressed anti-immigrant views.

Close to ten years after right-wing populism began its 21st-century ascent in the UK and the US, the same offer of affirmation to the un- or mis-recognised still regularly reoccurs. Recalling the Brexit leave campaign, at an "emergency press conference" in June 2024, Farage claimed that his return to UK electoral politics as leader of the Reform Party was necessary to speak up for those betrayed by Brexit (Farage, 2024). After channelling anti-immigrant feeling, he went on to speak directly to a particular group of voters:

But perhaps above all, what we're appealing to are those who are intending not to vote because they don't believe there is anybody within the Westminster establishment that actually stands up for them. Very often they are people running small businesses, acting as sole traders, they run a plumbing company, they run a taxi company, whatever it is. They know and they're right that no one in Westminster is on their side. Nobody in Westminster even understands what they do. (Farage, 2024)

The promise of recognition, of someone finally understanding and standing up, responds to, enacts and channels multiple already articulated economic and cultural grievances, together with barely articulated senses of something no longer feeling right. At the heart of its affective appeal is the promise that identities and ways of being will once again be valued and restored to their rightful status and position. As is now well acknowledged, right-wing populism articulates a felt loss of status and position, closely connected to the changing position of white masculinity amid the shifting racial and ethnic composition of the nation but also refracted through long term global economic shifts, including the intensification of precarity.

To reverse these felt losses, populism's promise of recognition begins with affirmation: that it is good and right to be a man, to be white, to be a conservative, to be patriotic, to be straight, to be a traditional wife or husband, to be working class, to live in a small town or rural area. Trump's redescription of 'a basket of deplorables' as 'wonderful and amazing people' performs this affirmation and the distinction from what is articulated as liberal neglect and contempt. His video addressing rioters on the day of the 6 January 2020 Capitol insurrection offered just such an affirmation. After claiming a 'fraudulent election', he asked his supporters to go home: 'We have to have peace. So go home, we love you, you're very special' (Relma et al., 2021).

The proposition that right-wing populism is an affirmative politics of recognition to 'forgotten men and women' (Trump, 2017) helps us understand the intensity of right-wing populist opposition to other forms of recognition. Right-wing populism, as it has blurred with contemporary conservatism, has involved an intense reaction to what commentators and politicians on the right claim are the excesses, at once dangerous and absurd, of a liberal, multi-cultural politics of recognition by inclusion. It is a response that recalls the history of other intense right-wing backlashes when minoritarian subjects demanded recognition (as in, 'political correctness gone mad', Peterson, 2018). The charge that animates the "war on woke" (especially as it is targeted to institutionalised concern with DEI [Diversity, Equality, and Inclusion]) is that recognition of ever finer social differences fragments the social, destroying shared norms, and undermining important sources of collective belonging and identification, principally those linked to the nation and family. Behind these claims, though, lurks resentment at subjects demanding "too much" or being given "too much", raising the spectre of a continual loss of status and pre-eminence for the entitled (white) subject. It is this threat that right-wing populism promises to end.

For one example, consider Eric Kaufman's recent book, *The Third Awokening*. Kaufman takes aim at what he terms 'progressive extremism'. Declaring 'wokeism' a 'cultural emergency', Kaufman lies the blame for this disastrous state of affairs squarely with liberals and their 'white guilt', even if the progressive left has supplied 'tactics'. In an advert for the book, he declares that 'Hyper sensitivity to minority feelings encourages people to be fragile rather than resilient, making it more likely that people will take offence, leading to more walking on eggshells, creating a vicious circle of victimhood culture' (Kaufman, 2024, np).

Critique of minoritarian subjects' liberal politics of recognition – and their feelings – is a feature, rather than blip, of the promise of the restoration of recognition to majoritarian subjects. Those who can't take the joke, who don't find it funny – that is, the 'feminist killjoys' and 'affect aliens' (Ahmed, 2010; 2024) – are not invited. When Farage, on the last day of the 2024 campaign, declared himself 'part of the same phenomena' as the misogynist influencer Andrew Tate, he noted their shared concern to counter the forces in society trying to 'stop young men from being young men' (Quinn, 2024). And there is nothing subtle about how women have been a prime target of Trump's cruelty throughout his public life. Indeed, Trump's misogyny has been called his 'one unwavering credo' (Gilbert, 2024). Not only does this overt embrace of misogyny affirm and recognise men who feel 'emasculated' (by economic hardship and by the rights of women to work and to their own bodies, etc.), but it marks out an exclusion: a zone of feeling accessible only to the selected, the seen.

While this is partly about securing fraying attachments to past promissory objects, as we set out in proposition three (*populism is optimistic*), the right's politics of recognition is more than an affirmation of majoritarian identities and ways of life as a backlash against minoritarian liberal claims to recognition, although it is partly that. Populism also grants a simple but powerful *absolution* alongside its politics of affirmation. It promises that you are not only 'wonderful and amazing' or 'very special', but you are also not responsible for the failures or difficulties in your life or in the life of whoever or whatever you value, be it family, place, or nation. Something else, something beyond yourself that you have no control over and did not consent to, is actually responsible. What that something else is varies. Its actual identity hardly matters. It goes by different names: the liberal elite, the woke, the metropolitan elite, the political establishment, the system, the liberal establishment, and so on. It can be found everywhere and anywhere: in the judiciary, in schools, in the BBC, in universities, in Hollywood, in *Dr Who*, in political parties, in the most successful "woke" global corporations, in the music of Taylor Swift, in Disney, even in the military. Occasionally, it takes form in particular political formations or institutions (the EU, Washington, Westminster, the Deep State, to name the main ones). What matters is that the something else is powerful, it is other to and outside you and those you care about and value, and it bears a responsibility that you do not.

Another way of saying this is that right-wing populism absolves subjects of responsibility for their predicament, or the present predicament of something they are attached to, such as the nation, group, or a place. As such, it breaks decisively with the responsibilisation of the self that has been so central to neoliberal and "advanced liberal" modes of governance (Lemke, 2001; Rose et al., 2006). This break is performed in and exemplified by Trump's final campaign advertisement for his 2016 presidential election (Trump, 2016). Midway through the advertisement it is clear where responsibility lies for the disastrous present Trump depicts, and it is not with individuals and their failure to become the right kind of consumer or investor, let alone a failure to work hard enough. Responsibility rests with: 'the elite that don't have your interests at heart' or the 'corrupt political establishment', as Trump's voiceover puts it, and is embodied in the figure of Hilary Clinton and other Democrat politicians. And these culprits are responsible for a lot: 'The political establishment who are trying to stop us is the same group responsible for our disastrous trade deals, massive illegal immigration, and economic and foreign policies that have bled our country dry.' The claim is followed by images of empty and shuttered factories, contrasted with intense activity elsewhere. Individuals are forced to endure this ruined present, but they bear no responsibility for it. Rather: 'It's a global power structure that is responsible for the economic decisions that have robbed our working class, stripped our country of its wealth, and put that money into the pockets of a handful of large corporations and political entities' (Trump, 2016).

Right-wing populism is, then, always a collective politics. It is built, first, from recognition and affirmation and, then, the redistribution of responsibility for the present injury that coexists with a sense of loss. The distinction between the people and its Other is a distinction between the injured and those responsible for the injury, as well as where the potential for change that breaks with the felt sense of loss is located. This partly explains why the reaction is so intense to minoritarian subjects who claim or demand recognition, as is exemplified in the ferocity of the "war on woke" or anti "DEI" movement. It is necessary for every populist politics to police the lines between the right and wrong kind of injured subject, between those who deserve more recognition than they presently feel, and those minoritised subjects who have taken or been given more than they deserve. To admit that other forms of injury exist and require redress is to undermine the exclusionary constitution of "the people" along heteropatriarchal, white lines. What matters is the injury of the people who have been mis or non-recognised. Trump's comments on 6 January addressed to rioters are exemplary: 'I know your pain. I know you're hurt. We had an election that was stolen from us' (Trump quoted by Liptak, 2021).

By making recognition of injury for some and the denial of injury for others central to its affective appeal, right-wing populism is best understood as post-liberal, rather than simply performing a decisive break with liberalism. With liberalism, it begins from the importance of recognition to contemporary political subjectivity, as well as the centrality of injury to ways of performing contemporary subjecthood. This extends all the way to populist leaders. At an election address in Washington in June 2024, and as he talked about his persecution and prosecution, Trump performed a wounded subjectivity, alongside the sense of fun that, as we'll see below, is also a feature of right-wing populism's excess: 'And I have the wounds all over my body. If I took this shirt off you'd see a beautiful, beautiful person ... but you'd see wounds all over me. I've taken a lot of wounds, I can tell you. More than I suspect any president ever' (Trump, 2024a).

But right-wing populism is "post" liberal in the sense that it is not based on the same process of conditional inclusion that characterises 'the passions of recognition' that late liberalism works through (Povinelli, 2002: 17). Instead of performing inclusivity, populism induces an explicit cut that casts some people out of the empty-full term "the people". Populism requires a public line to be drawn between "the people" and its Other, even if the contents of these categories might shift. There must be something other than the people that serves as cause for the injury, and can thereafter, as we'll see, become the object of resentment compelling mixtures of anger, hate, and contempt. By invoking the unitary "people", populism brings about an antagonistic front between the people and an "other": 'a *them* that is designated as not only *not* "the people", but as its film negative; an image of what society should not be, providing the movement with much of its affective impetus' (Salter, 2016: 117).

Through this affirmative politics of recognition and the constitution of an antagonistic front, another affirmation follows – 'wonderful, amazing people' who feel various kinds of loss and injury are right to feel resentment. The populist leader promises: You are right in your feelings of dispossession and loss. Your country has changed and you don't recognise it, you cannot speak freely anymore, you work hard but don't see the rewards. You who are most authentic, most wonderful, are now being treated like the Other, a stranger in the strange land you once belonged to. Your many grievances are valid. Whatever the grievance is and wherever it is directed, it is right and correct because the real Other has stolen something from you or received something it doesn't deserve. And it has been helped to do so by the same "elites" or "political establishment" who have forgotten or abandoned or neglected you and are responsible for your injury and loss. With this affirmation, the excessive gestures and displays of populism not only bolster (often authoritarian) leaders, but they also introduce a feeling of agency, an intensified feeling of personal sovereignty, into the realm of formal politics. The affirmed subject of populism is capable of action, even insurrection. You are right to "stop the steal", as the election was stolen by the establishment.

Put differently, right-wing populism encourages and celebrates resentment, in ways that, as Brown (2019: 177) argues, undoes the distinction between the 'rage of the economically left behinds' and 'dethroned white masculinism'. Lawrence Rosenthal's (2020) description of global right-wing populism as an 'empire of resentment' is apt. The resentment is prolific, gathering around two objects that come to be inseparable in their position as other to the people, as both Brown and Rosenthal convincingly demonstrate. First, to the minoritarian Other who is recognised and appears to win and, second, to the "elite" or "establishment", or whichever term is being used, that bestows recognition upon the Other and has forgotten or abandoned or has contempt for the "very special people" who deserve recognition.

The bellicosity that courses through right-wing populism, and appears close to being its affective signature, is a necessary part of this ressentiment-infused post-liberal affirmative politics of recognition. The particularity of the right's post-liberal politics of recognition is that it affirms the righteousness of anger and hatred, of the contempt and rage directed towards the bad Others.

The Other is multiple: trans people, LGBTQ+ communities, Black Lives Matter, The Woke, protestors against genocide and for Palestinian statehood, Globalists, women who were part of the #MeToo movement, the "Squad", footballers who "take the knee", and on and on. But it is in relation to immigration and immigrants that the bellicosity that is a structural feature of right-wing populism (and the most internationally consistent element) has been performed particularly intensely, with anti-immigrant feeling central to all variants of UK and US right-wing populisms over the past fifteen years.

Farage's return to UK politics as leader was accompanied by his claim that 2024 was the "immigration election". Speaking after a period of asylum-related policy in the UK defined by its combination of performative cruelty and the intentional production of destitution (Darling, 2022), Farage in his "emergency press conference" decried the 'massive betrayal' of the 17.4 million people who had voted for Brexit. In an increasingly bellicose tone, he made clear the real emergency that had drawn him back to UK electoral politics on behalf of the "betrayed":

> It's actually about our country and its people. And we're worried, and we're fearful, of many of the impacts we've seen. We find what happened after those local elections just a few weeks ago. Candidates winning in Leeds, Burnley, Bradford and elsewhere, standing, shouting Al Akbar, standing, shouting 'we are coming to get you'. The birth of sectarian politics in our country, caused by massively irresponsible immigration policies. And it was the Labour Party that opened the door. And who would have believed a conservative party would have accelerated it. (Farage, 2024)

Anti-immigrant resentment and rage and anger is amplified in Trump's 2024 presidential campaign, with its emphasis on retribution for the injuries delivered to Trump and his supporters. Recalling the promise to "build the wall" in the 2016 campaign and his claim that Mexico was sending murderers and rapists across the border, his 2024 campaign centres what he regularly terms "the invasion". At a campaign rally in Nevada, the start of his rambling speech focused on immigration, the lack of border security, and "Crooked" Joe Biden:

> Under Biden the invasion is just a disaster what's happening. It's never happened like this, in less than four years crooked Joe has imported more illegal aliens into our country than at any other time than in the history of our country times. Maybe 50. There's never been anything like this happening to our country. They're changing the fabric of our country. They're destroying our country. They're doing things that are unthinkable. This open border. So many bad things, but this open border situation where you're allowing millions and millions of people to flood our country, we can't handle it. No country could handle it, it's not sustainable. The entire world is emptying their prisons and jails, insane asylums and mental institutions. (Trump, 2024b)

Who Trump is referring to when he talks about what "they're" doing is a little unclear, not only because of the rambling, barely coherent monologue punctuated with laughter lines and familiar refrains. It could be immigrants, President Joe Biden, or perhaps the countries supposedly sending people. All mix together as resentment is translated into other-oriented bellicosity, and the punitive promise of deportation and imprisonment (in a way that recalls the promise to "stop the boats" in the UK). But during his anti-immigrant diatribe, and in the midst of the laughter that coexists with anger and rage, Trump changed tone. He paused for a moment and recalled Clinton's "deplorables" comment some eight years earlier, celebrating how "we", his supporters and him, had turned the phrase into a "positive thing".

Proposition 2: Populism Is Excessive

Populism was always linked to a dangerous excess, which puts the clear-cut moulds of a rational community into question. (Laclau 2005: x)

Whether it is in the bellicosity of anti-immigrant rhetoric or the affirmation of *very* special people, right-wing populism is characterised by its affective excess. Trump's campaign rallies mix combative, other-orientated hatred with humour and exaggeration, including the violent "fun" of mocking the marginalised and promising to punish his opponents and the vulnerable alike. At first glance, the Trumpian spectacle of excess, the lengthy, rambling rallies in which the leader performs for the pleasure of the crowd, is an effervescence of right-wing populism not seen in the UK. And yet, there are circuits and confluences. In February 2024, when conservative former UK Prime Minister Liz Truss appeared side by side with Nigel Farage at the American Conservative Political Action Conference

(CPAC) 'swapping conspiracy theories on stage with [America] right-wing populists', one American journalist noted the dissonance of this convergence: '[T]he distance between the MAGA hat-wearing Trump fans in Maryland and the gray suits of Tory Party conference in Britain can be measured in cultural light-years' (Blewett, 2024).

Yet it is perhaps this very greyness that populism in the UK promises a respite from. Four months later, when Farage, announced that he would stand in the general election for Reform UK, his entrance did not so much shift the race as challenge the tone of it. As he pledged to lead a "people's revolt" against the "establishment", in June 2024, Farage also promised another political passion to add to anti-immigrant bellicosity and recognition of loss: fun. 'We think this election needs a bit of gingering up', he remarked at his emergency press conference. 'Thus far it is the dullest, most boring campaign we have ever seen in our lives. And it's funny because the more the two big party leaders try to be different, the more they actually sound the same' (Farage, 2024). As John Crace wrote for *The Guardian*, 'Nigel Farage is the only politician who appears to be enjoying himself. Everyone else is comatose or terminally depressed. Where is the joy?' (Crace, 2024).

What to make of this offer of affective difference, of an excess that aspires to break with the muted tones, the disaffection, of "there is no alternative"? By *excess* we refer to a disruptive supplement over what is expected or anticipated within a given situation. We prefer this term rather than others more closely tied to a pre-existing norm, such as subversion or transgression, because it allows us to remain open about how "excess" sometimes appears in the service of norms while at other times as part of their overturning. Excess is also apropos because it is linked to the concept of enjoyment, especially as it exceeds what is comfortable or able to be assimilated into an established order (of the self or society) (Zizek, 2002). The proposition that *populism is excessive* centres how this quality is performed, how it circulates, and how its capacity to both attract and repel works to constitute and differentiate a populist structure of feeling.

Populism's excess activates a longstanding ambivalence in Western political thought about the role of passion, emotion, or feelings in politics, and especially as manifest by "the masses". In *On Populist Reason* (2005), Ernesto Laclau shows how theories of 'the crowd' have historically worked to delegitimise popular politics in the West. By setting 'rational forms of social organization' in counter-distinction to 'mass phenomena', 19th and 20th century political and social theorists expressed their wariness of the masses, whom they deemed too emotional and unpredictable for political enfranchisement (Laclau, 2005: 29). Populism, when cast as an existential threat to liberal democracy, takes up the mantel of the irrational political "other" inherited over the long durée of Western thought, traversing the centuries from Plato's intemperate "democratic type" on through Gustav le Bon's 19th-century deluded masses, Elias Canetti's mid-20th-century devouring crowd, and what Douglas Kellner calls the *American Nightmare* (2016: 54), in which 'Trump was the *vox populi* of his follower's [sic] fears and rage'.

That populism is excessive precisely in how it exceeds the bureaucratic rationalities of liberal democratic institutions appears frequently in the public discourse that eddies around it. In the context of mounting political tensions and a crisis of futurity in the West, the populist drive that propelled Britain out of the EU and landed Trump in the White House, not once but twice, appears as a threat to the rational administration of government: a dangerous excess, fuelled by fluctuations of passion and people's readiness to believe anything under conditions of doubt and uncertainty. While a suspicion of danger may cling to populism, it is also true that the threat of right-wing populism to liberal democracy in the 21st century is, in fact, verifiable. Populist governments in Hungary, Turkey, and Brazil have actively worked to roll-back democracy by undermining or dismantling key democratic institutions, protections, and constitutional frameworks (Mounk and Kyle, 2018). Yet the *excess* of populism should not be conflated with the political agendas of populist leaders. In many cases, the political programs of these leaders are directly authoritarian, with populism indicating a tonal quality rather than an agenda.

The excess of populism manifests in what is over-the-top about how the populist leader presents himself to the public eye. From the official proclamation that Trump 'unequivocally, will be the healthiest individual ever elected to the presidency' ahead of his victory in the 2016 election (Cassidy, 2018), to Boris Johnson boasting that he was 'fit as a butcher's dog' and 'bursting with antibodies' after being forced to self-quarantine in November 2020 (Johnson, 2020a), performances of over-pumped masculine virility exceed what is called for (e.g. a bill of health or quarantine routines). Underlining the robust, masculine physicality of the populist leader resonates with how Vladimir Putin presents himself (bare chested, on horse, with tiger) and more broadly with how authoritarian populist leaders around the world promise protection from imagined forces of "masculine decline" and the threatening ascendance of racialised or otherwise minoritarian others – 'demographic fantasies' that appear with the intensity and lack of coherence of 'fever dreams' (Gökarıksel et al., 2019: 562).

Excess also appears in dramatically staged events, such as when on 1 June 2020 Trump chose to respond to the demonstrations erupting across the country in protest of the police murder of George Floyd with a photo op in front of the historic St John's Episcopal Church. The president's walk across the street from the White House was ushered by defence secretary Mark Esper's command to 'dominate the battle space' of the DC protesters, and it resulted in the use of rubber bullets, tear gas, and a Black Hawk helicopter flying low enough 'to snap tree limbs and tear signs from the sides of buildings, a show-of-force manoeuvre often seen in combat zones to scare off insurgents' (Tan et al., 2020: n.p.; Flegenheimer, 2020). The sheer lack of necessity for any of this – for the photo op itself, let alone for the escalation of state violence against the peaceful demonstrators – was not incidental to the event but its most significant content.

On a different register, we might think of a campaign video for the conservatives in the 2019 general election as similarly excessive, but this time invoking the absurd and playful. Featuring Boris Johnson at a bakery in the midlands, he made a pie and put it in the oven. Smiling, with sleeves rolled up and a baker's apron on, Johnson asserted his promise of an 'oven ready deal' to resolve the Brexit impasse. Like Trump's photo op, though less immediately violent, the oven ready skit was entirely uncalled for, excessive. It clarified nothing. The performance implies that what needs to be explained is not how Johnson is going to deliver a Brexit deal, but what it means for something to be "oven ready" – a phrase chosen specifically because everyone knows exactly what it means.

The harmlessness of the baking exercise in the UK contrasts to the violent removal of peaceful protestors in the US, and certainly this divergence is significant politically and practically. Yet our contention is that the shared *excessiveness* is also significant. The excess appears beyond utility, beyond what is necessary. It fosters a sense of more or less violent, more or less knowingly playful, difference from other politics and other politicians. In both cases, the affective register of politics departs from ordinary comforts and satisfactions to become decidedly more disruptive (Hook, 2017; see also Glynos and Stavrakakis, 2008; Jutel, 2018; Salter, 2016). Moreover, there is an inbuilt logic of escalation. What excites interest and provokes a feeling of politics-not-as-usual one time will not be able to do that again. During the 2012 Olympics when Boris Johnson, then mayor of London, got stuck on a zip wire and was suspended over Victoria Park, ruffled and absurd with a Union Jack in each hand, even the sceptical recognised it as a counterintuitive triumph. In the words of one observer, 'If Boris Johnson was ever going to have a golden age, that was probably it. God help us' (Addley, 2019). Yet by 2024, when the Liberal Democrats erected a giant hourglass to represent 'time running out for Rishi Sunak', dressed an activist up as a 'Tory dinosaur', and had their leader, Ed Davey, fall off a paddleboard to highlight England's sewage crisis, the stunts lacked the disruptive frisson of Johnson's antics, felt more utilitarian. In case it was not clear how the stunt at the lake was supposed to *feel*, Davey ploddingly explained to the press that he had just kept falling in, 'But it's fun' (Rawlinson, 2024).

The question is, fun for whom? Key to the populist structure of feeling is that the froth of populist excess does not arise only from the performances of leaders. Populism is a site of excessive passion for followers even more centrally than leaders, who may catalyse these feelings but whose passion alone is insufficient. Whether evident in the ardent proliferation of Q-Anon theories or in the 'near spiritual devotion' said to be lavished upon Trump by his supporters (Wilkie, 2020), the sense that populists both enjoy their leader's excess and are themselves excessive colours the atmosphere of the populist surge in the US and the UK.

While there are countless examples that could be used to illustrate the intensity of Trump supporters, one such video went viral on 4 November 2020, the day following the election

(Insider Paper, 2020). The video shows a press conference in which election officials outside the Clark County Election Center in Nevada are reporting on the vote count when they are interrupted by a man wearing a 'BBQ, Beer, Freedom' tank top. The man lunges onto camera yelling, 'The Biden crime family steals this election! The media is covering it up! The Biden crime family steals this election! The media is covering it up! We won our freedom for the world. Give us our freedom Joe Biden! Joe Biden is covering up this election! He's stealing it!' Having yelled himself hoarse and not been interrupted or forced to leave, the man turns and walks away. The press conference resumes. One reporter can be heard asking, 'Where were we?'. The spectacle is one in which the excess of the man's fist-pumping, sweaty anger becomes absurd precisely because it is not met with any return of passion but instead left to fizzle out. The man runs out of slogans to shout and leaves. The mundane workings of the Clark County office prevail, it seems, over the threatening excess of populist fervour and vacuity.

In displaying the 'BBQ, Beer, Freedom' man as an aberration at the press conference, from one perspective the video delegitimises the populist actor along the classic lines of Western political thought: he appears to be irrational in the face of the rational proceedings of democratic bureaucracy. And yet, while amusing to anti-Trump viewers, it is unlikely that such a performance embarrasses the actor himself, who accomplished his intervention. What happened and what was said was exactly what was intended. While the cameras focus on the affective energy of the Trump supporter, questions about the evidence for the claims (of a stolen election, a Biden crime family) are deferred. The righteous rage of 'BBQ, Beer, Freedom' brooks no further discussion.

If the scene-stealers are expressing justified *anger*, the dogged accusation that right-wing populism gains its traction by fuelling racism and white supremacy becomes just another sign of how "the people" are misunderstood and demonised. Emphasising justified anger, *The Financial Times* published an article in its book review section in January 2020 titled 'Populism and the Smoldering Rage of American Poverty' that presented 'new books [that] counter the view of populist voters as racist. They're just angry – and rightly so' (Luce, 2020). The argument is that if there are racists in the ranks (and even if Trump overtly embraces neo-Nazi groups and their signs) this should not be mistaken for the *content* of right-wing populism but something extra – the excess of the excess, one could say. Racism, in other words, appears as an effervescence within the right-wing populist structure of feeling, where it operates as both a mode of (transgressive) enjoyment and a reaction to a perceived "theft of enjoyment" – that is, to the threat of a usurper (migrants, women, non-white subjects) enjoying in one's place, sitting on one's throne (Lacan, 1990; Hook, 2017).

Some of those who thrill to populism's affirmations and promises may have become swept up *despite*, not because of, the drumbeat of nativism and white supremacy. This capacity for attraction was suggested in the aftermath of Trump's 2024 victory, when it became clear that he had gained support from Black and Hispanic voters. Under the ever-widening populist umbrella, overt or conscious racism may internally differentiate its evolving structure of feeling, variegating its unfolding. And yet, the association between right-wing populism and racism is not spurious but a consistent part of its expression (not just in the US and the UK but globally). Many have shown that Trump and his allies have knowingly and strategically embraced racism and xenophobia to enflame and affirm white voters. As Jonathan Chait wrote in *New York Magazine* early in Trump's first term, 'Race is the unifying idea Trump has used to recast not only his party's place within the country but his country's place in the world. It is where his administration has been most passionate – and also most effective' (Chait, 2017). When racist comments percolated through the campaigns of multiple Reform candidates during the 2024 election season and an activist was caught on camera using a racist slur against Rishi Sunak, Nigel Farage distanced himself from these views. Yet whatever he said and whatever he intended, it was widely reported when the first question an audience member asked Farage on the 2024 BBC's 'Question Time: Leaders' Special' was, 'What is it about your party that attracts racists?' (Whannel 2024).

In its power to excite, the excess of populism can attract even those who are repelled by it. This is apparent in arguments in favour of a left populism. For example, suggesting that the cancellation of liberal-democratic futures is a result of liberalism's bloodlessness, Mouffe writes, 'The mistake of liberal rationalism is to ignore the affective dimension mobilised by collective identifications and to imagine that those supposedly archaic "passions" are bound to disappear with the advance of individualism and the progress of rationality' (Mouffe, 2005: 6). From this perspective, the white man in the 'BBQ, Beer, Freedom' tank top appears to have something that the vote counting officials do not: an affective dimension of political identification. Consequently, Mouffe (2018: 82) suggests, 'In the struggle to establish a new hegemonic formation' – that is, if one is to effectively counter the interruption that wins even as it loses – 'it is essential to adopt a "populist" strategy.'

The left's fascination with populist passion brings into focus the broader issue of enjoyment in politics – specifically, the question of whether, and how, enjoyment functions as a political factor (Žižek, 2002; see Luger (2024) on 'authoritarian joy'). Populist enjoyment takes on a distinctly sadistic cast, going beyond what has been called the cruelty of conservative politics (e.g. targeting the homeless, reducing aid to the poor, and create purposefully hostile environments for migrants) to introduce an excess, a full-throated appetite for others' suffering (Matheson, 2022; Serwer, 2018). On this register, the excesses of populism signal an obscene enjoyment rooted in the "violent delights" of white supremacy, militarism, and conspiracy theory – an enjoyment that liberals and progressives overtly wish not to enjoy but rather to deflate. On the other hand, this populist excess may arise from what Laclau and Mouffe see as the properly political passion of assembling "the people", an enjoyment that some contend the left *must* embrace if it is to establish a political (hegemonic) power able to counter the excesses of the right (Laclau,2005; Mouffe, 2018; Stavrakakis, 2007). In other words, populism's excess can be both what differentiates its structure of feeling, making it inaccessible to those who refuse or are excluded from its "enjoyments", and that which makes it an implacable political force capable of dispersing its feeling-structure ever more widely – for example, in the rise since 2023 of an explicitly antiimmigrant left in Germany and Denmark.

But perhaps even more disconcerting than how liberal and left observers hover between discomfort and desire in the face of populist excess is the work that placing obscene enjoyment on the side of right-wing populism does to *allow the enjoyment of liberal democracy to remain unseen*. For the problem of equating populism with passion is not only that populism exceeds the discourse on its emotionality by operating according to its own (submerged) rationalities. But also, such analysis runs the risk of ignoring how "liberal rationalism" is supported by its own disavowed enjoyments – in, for example, the masculinism, ablism, and white-supremacy that dully prop up its "neutral" institutions. Consider the flash of joy that energised exhausted liberal and progressive US-election watchers when CNN announced on 6 November that 'national defense airspace has been put in place over Democratic nominee Joe Biden's home in Wilmington, Delaware' (Muntean, 2020), thereby demonstrating the overwhelming force of the US military apparatus taking its place behind the newly elected president. What disavowed attachment to US militarism did this flutter of elation betray? One might consider David Hook's (2017: 609) well-taken argument that there is no "good *jouissance*" for the left, but that does not mean that the left does not enjoy. It is possible that populism is not exceptional for its excess of passion, but that its passion is exceptionally troubling, even unsightly, for those who distrust not only the end game of specific (right-wing populist) passions but also political enjoyment tout court.

The proposition that populism is excessive is like a pitfall trap. Baited with the Western-historical ideal of the rational political subject, it delivers its unwitting target to a confrontation with their own enjoyment and its lack. And yet, if one avoids the cul-de-sacs of condemning populism for its unseemliness, desiring it for its promise of "more", or attempting to harness its passions in cold blood, one may still be able to feel one's way forward into the living processes of populist feeling. One way to do this is by going back. Back to what has been "left behind" in the impasse of the fractured present, where populist feelings loop around from the past to the future, promising that things will be good – even great – again. For this final move we turn to our third proposition.

Proposition 3: Populism Is Optimistic

On 6 October 2020, Boris Johnson delivered a virtual speech to the first conservative party conference since their general election victory in December 2019 (Johnson, 2020b). Shifting from the topic of COVID-19, perhaps to divert attention from criticisms of his handling of the pandemic and reenergise support for his "people's government", he directly addressed the increasingly contested topic of the country's relation with the past. The immediate context was the Black Lives Matter protests. In an intensifying "culture war" fuelled by a right-wing backlash to those protests, what was at stake, for right-wing populists, was who storied the nation and whether and how people should attach to pasts. Johnson distinguished himself and the Conservative Party from a caricature of the protests. He stressed: 'We are proud of this country's culture and history and traditions; they [referring to the "Labour opposition"] literally want to pull statues down, to re-write the history of our country, to edit our national CV to make it look more politically correct.' Amid a manufactured outrage surrounding the BBC's supposed decision not to sing the lyrics to 'Rule Britannia' at their Last Night of the Proms event and in a style that mixed irony and exaggeration, he stressed that, as Conservatives: 'We aren't embarrassed to sing old songs about how Britannia rules the waves.'

Some weeks earlier, Trump had made similar remarks about the relation to the national past during his seemingly stuttering re-election campaign at a hastily rearranged 'White House Conferences on American History'. In typically bellicose terms presumably designed to energise a base concerned with the ebbing privileges of whiteness and felt threats to white supremacy, he stressed that: 'We must clear away the twisted web of lies in our schools and classrooms and teach our children the magnificent truth about our country. We want our sons and daughters to know that they are the citizens of the most exceptional nation in the history of the world'(Trump, 2020b).

While offered in their partially connected but different affective styles, Johnson and Trump's speeches exemplified how during a "culture war" right-wing populism gives people permission to feel pride in threatened objects/scenes. People are given permission to attach to intensely reasserted national stories and permission to not feel shame at a time of intense reckoning with pasts. The affective grounds for this reassertion are interconnected structures of feeling which, while distinct, hold various almost-lost pasts in suspension, making them both problematic *and* available to be reactivated through populist political projects and campaigns. In the UK, for example, Paul Gilroy (2004: 111) highlights the existence of what he terms postcolonial and postimperial melancholia, based on 'Britain's inability to mourn its loss of empire and accommodate to Empire's consequences … '. We could speculate that a different form of racialised melancholia exists in the US but focused on the inability to mourn the white supremacist liberal order built on slavery amid continued attachments to the American dream.[2] What is so striking about Gilroy's account is that he stresses the 'odd combination' or 'unstable mixture' of feelings which form a melancholic relation – 'a signature

---

[2] See Daniel Martinze Hosang and Joseph Lowndes (2019) on how Trump's 'racial populism' (p. 67) takes up longstanding right-wing discourses of the undeserving poor (e.g. 'parasites') to differentiate 'those groups deemed self-reliant, autonomous, and worthy of social protection from those who are dependent, debased, and worthy of abandonment and disavowal' (p. 4). This right-wing discourse of deservingness obscures both the failure of the promises of the American Dream and the role that racism has played historically and continues to play in propping up the myth of equal opportunity in the US.

combination of manic elation with misery, self-loathing and ambivalence' (Gilroy, 2004: 114). The result is that public issues concerning race and ethnicity are enveloped by unstable mixtures of surprise and denial, ambivalence and hostility.

There are other similar structures of feeling. Lauren Berlant (2011) identifies the continued but fraying attachment to the post-war Fordist settlement in the US, or rather the heteronormative good life fantasies which accompanied and animated it. In naming 'cruel optimism' as the maintenance of attachment to objects/scenes which have become 'problematic' because of their 'compromised' conditions of possibility, she explicitly distinguishes cruel optimism from the desire to temporalise a loss which, for her, characterises melancholia (and Gilroy shows never quite happens in the UK in relation to imperialism or colonialism). Despite this difference, what these various diagnoses give us is a sense of the present as over-full of problematic objects/scenes of attachment which produce something like a stalled present, held between residual past attachments and the slow cancellation of the future. As structures of feeling, both postcolonial/post-imperial melancholia and cruel optimism are ways in which past objects/scenes associated with national pre-eminence remain residual parts of the present. Even if relations to them are complicated, as Gilroy reminds us when he emphasises the 'odd' combination of feelings surrounding race, or Berlant when they write of the tension between objects/scenes which sustain and harm, they are nevertheless available to serve as the representational and affective material of right-wing populism.

In relation to these affective conditions, right-wing populism translates an object/scene of potential loss into an occasion for attachment. For us, this translation defines the specificity of right-wing populism: the restoration of an unruined past in a disruptive future to come.[3] As part of the affirmative but resentment-infused politics of recognition, various actors internal and external to the nation and standing in opposition to "the people" are invoked as the forces that have, to date, hindered the nation from progressing toward or reclaiming the virtues embodied by its past. Trump was most explicit about this in his 2020 re-election campaign, articulating it in strikingly bellicose terms, amid a story of betrayal and threat in the present:

Left-wing mobs have torn down statues of our founders, desecrated our memorials, and carried out a campaign of violence and anarchy. Far-left demonstrators have chanted the words "America was never great." The left has launched a vicious and violent assault on law enforcement – the universal symbol of the rule of law in America. These radicals have been aided and abetted by liberal politicians, establishment media, and even large corporations. (Trump, 2020b)

If offered with less bellicosity and without the same conspiratorial tone, a similar cast of characters animated Johnson's narrative of his 'people's government' standing in opposition

---

[3] This makes the optimism of right-wing populism different to forms of optimism organised around ideals and ideas of 'progress', in which a better future overcomes and erases the near and far past in a movement of perpetual betterment. It also raises the question of how the optimism of right-wing populism relates to the optimism of forms of non-populist conservative thought, noting that not all are based on either the politics of return we outline below or the politics of progressive betterment. We might think of optimisms founded on the continuation of something valued through past, present and future in which optimism is grounded in the supposedly timeless.

to 'liberal elites', 'do-gooder lawyers', etc. The promise of right-wing populism is that neither the object/scene nor the attachment is compromised … a*s long as whatever is responsible for compromising the relation in the near-past is defeated and the sovereignty of "the people" restored* (whether that be "elites", "liberal do-gooders", "illegal immigrants", "the EU", "China", and so on). In other words, populism promises that the future has not been cancelled, the object of attachment *is still good*; there is no "bad object", but only bad "others" usurping and degrading the scene of attachment.

Populism is a politics of the return, not least the restoration of recognition. The future politics of populism is a denial of the future, if by "future" we mean the modernist time of openness and the new. This future is erased in an endless temporal loop whereby the good past becomes the hoped-for better future, with the promise that the immediate past will be negated and transcended. We could say, to develop this argument, that right-wing populism is a symptom of the 'cancellation of the future' (Berardi, 2011) we described in the introduction in a very straightforward way: because images of a different and better future are exhausted, what is left are lingering almost but not quite lost images of pasts, yoked to the available affective catalyst and empty signifier "the people". The only resources left to construct futures are the remnants of past presents kept just about alive in nostalgia, and structures of feeling such as postcolonial/postimperial melancholia and cruel optimism. We could go further and say right-wing populism is not simply symptomatic of the cancellation of the future, but another mechanism for that cancellation. For in articulating the future as the return of the past, in investing optimism in that return, even if often framed as a disruption of the present, the modernist future that animated so many progressive political movements is confirmed as lost.

There is clearly a lot to the diagnosis that the optimism of right-wing populism is anchored in the promise of a return to a lost or threatened national pre-eminence in which the ebbing privileges of whiteness will be restored. This means that right-wing populism is structured around a cyclical rather than linear temporality. While the political content and aims are completely different, we might place right-wing populism in the context of other ways in which the relation between past, present, and future has recently been unsettled. As we shall see in the next chapter, recent progressive political movements also insist on the necessity of returning to the past but to enable reckoning or reparation for the violences that accumulated alongside and enabled the modernist promise of progress. Put simply, publics have sparked into being around the past in a way that renders the relation between past and present a matter and scene of public contestation. As well as the cancellation of the future, a second context for the emergence of right-wing populism would, then, be intensifying efforts to destabilise settled and invested pasts. During this uncertainty and the making of the past into a sphere of contestation, the promise of right-wing populism is not only of a return to the past but, more importantly, to restabilise the once hegemonic affect-imbued meaning of increasingly publicly contested national pasts – as we saw in the Johnson and Trump speeches.

To summarise this argument, we could say that right-wing populism re-establishes an optimistic attachment to objects/scenes of nationalist feeling. By "optimistic" we do not mean an attachment that necessarily feels good, although of course it may, particularly when connected to promises to restore dignity and recognition to those who feel their absence from "elites", and the lures of excess enjoyment. Rather, and after Berlant (2011), we consider an optimistic attachment to be one where the object/scene promises something that is necessary, or the subject or group feels and thinks is necessary, for their continuation and/or their flourishing. As Berlant puts it, optimism involves a '... sustaining inclination to return to the scene of fantasy that enables you to expect that this time, nearness to this thing will help you or a world to become different in just the right way' (Berlant, 2011: 2). More precisely, right-wing populism makes previously fragile objects/scenes *unproblematic* – that is, something that does not provoke scrutiny or disagreements – in two ways. First, they counter any actual or perceived shaming or mocking of attachments, as expressed most intensely in the recent eruption of "culture wars" and the backlash to Black Lives Matter. What right-wing populism makes available through the "time loop" of a return which refuses the new futures a present reckoning might enable is a stable and positive relation to the object/scene. People can once again unambivalently attach to objects/scenes of past national pre-eminence and be recognised and valued for doing so. Second, right-wing populism promises that the conditions for the realisation of the object/scene are *no longer compromised*. "The people" becomes the means through which the good life fantasy can be realised. As faith in other grounds for optimism wanes, "the people" resurges as the route to a better future, made present through the excessiveness of right-wing populism.

This diagnosis is the inverse of Berlant's. Berlant (2011) tracks dramas of adjustment amid the *dissolution* of optimistic objects/scenes that held space for good life fantasies, many of which originated in the Fordist settlement. Theirs is a diagnosis of what happens to the forms of liberal optimism based on progressive betterment which were articulated through Fordist good life fantasies. Scenes/objects have become 'problematic' because their conditions of possibility are 'compromised'. People's adjustment doesn't change the fact they are compromised. It is at best a slightly less desperate holding on. Perhaps the promise that right-wing populism offers is that *no adjustment is necessary.* That the scenes/objects of the present might still be stabilised, might still hold space open for a series of conventional good life fantasies. We would hesitate before determining whether this optimism is *cruel* for those in the relation – in the specific sense that Berlant uses the phrase to articulate how 'the very vitalising or animating potency of an object/scene of desire contributes to the attrition of the very thriving that is supposed to be made possible by the work of attachment in the first place' (Berlant, 2011: 25). Perhaps we need to think of a variety of different optimisms, cruel and otherwise, that are entangled with right-wing populisms?[4] We could, instead, stress that the optimism of right-wing populism is 'cruel' to those who are determined to be outside of "the people" – who must be reduced and devalued and, potentially, subject to material as well as symbolic violence if the better future is to return. In this way populism's optimism underscores the inclusion of some and exclusion of others from its promise.

In order to achieve its promised future, populism calls for a break with the present and near past. Consider Trump's vision of the future of America in his January 2017 inauguration speech (Trump, 2017). Invoking an image of a dystopian present

---

[4] Berlant is ambivalent on the question of whether all optimisms are cruel but settles on the position that some optimisms are crueller than others (Berlant, 2011: 24/25). This makes the cruelty or not of optimism the defining matter for distinguishing between forms of optimism. For us, as important is the relation with the future (and thus past and present) which different optimisms are organised around.

that featured 'mothers and children trapped in poverty in our inner cities' and 'factories scattered like tombstones', Trump went on to promise that what has been lost will be brought back: 'America will start winning again, winning like never before.' Jobs, borders, wealth, and dreams will all be 'brought back', a return to a better past. If Trump's vision enacts residual attachments to Fordism, Johnson's address immediately after his general election victory in December 2019 involves a similar attachment to the sovereign nation (Johnson, 2019). As with Trump, an intense, decisive break from the near past is necessary, mostly because of the actions of 'politicians' who have 'squandered' time with 'squabbles about Brexit'. Leaving the European Union is the break from the present and near past that will result in 'taking back control of our laws, borders, money, our trade, immigration system'. From this break, after the resolution promised in the slogan 'Get Brexit Done' and amid the resurgence of a fantasy of national sovereignty around a supposedly lost 'control', a different future opens, one which yokes fantasies of sovereignty to a key element of the post-war settlement and national imaginary – the NHS, 'a single beautiful idea' – mixed with a host of images of progress and world-besting. From policing and immigration to schools and green technology, 'We'll do it'.

The reasons for the necessity of the break vary, but what is common across Trump and Johnson's speeches is that even as they promise a return to mythical lost glory, they stress disruptive discontinuity with the present and recent past. Indeed, while Berlant focuses on the difficult work of enabling continuity in the objects/scenes of attachment in the midst of dissolution, critical work has often valued hope as an occasion of *discontinuity* (see Anderson et al., 2020). Likewise, right-wing populism promises a break after the reckoning with the "elite", who are responsible for the damaged or compromised world: that something will end, that what has become "normal" will not continue. It is after the "break" that the good future, corresponding in part to the lost past of pre-eminence, will arise.

Populism's promised future is not quite the future of progress, the time of linear transparent betterment. Neither is it the knowable future, the rational, predictable and this programmable future. Unlike the future of progress, right-wing populist optimism is always fragile, always without guarantees, because of the actions of various actors who are external to and act against "the people". Furthermore, the relation with the future cannot have the linearity of progress or prediction because there must always be disruptive discontinuity. Chronological time must be interrupted, a break must happen, disruption is necessary. Neither, though, is the future of right-wing populism the open future as advocated and practised across the 'freedom dreams' (Kelley, 2002) of radical groups, where the aim is to bring into being other, radically different worlds. The temporality of rupture, an interruption and disavowal of the present and near-past, is accompanied by a return to the lost but better past in the future, together with ready to hand images of a better future (often crouched in terms of infrastructure, reactivating the relation between infrastructure and modernity). In this sense, populist futures happen after the double cancellation of the future – where both the future as scene of progress and scene of novelty are no longer available. Rupture and return sustain the optimism which coexists with the emptiness and excessiveness which are right-wing populism.

Conclusion: Populism Emergent?

Propositions are contestable. They open onto a changing present, temporarily holding something still. They are always issued from a place and a time, the boundaries of which are never given, as new tendencies and trajectories knit and fold past and future affective presents together. We finished the first draft of what has become this chapter in the strange days in late December 2020 and early January 2021 when Trump desperately clung to office after his election loss, a transitional period of intensified uncertainty preceded by feverish speculation about how and whether Trump would exit, bookended by the mediated spectacle of insurrection in the Capitol. While the events of 6 January 2021 in the Capitol have since found their genre (indeed in this chapter we have repeated the now dominant naming of it as an insurrection), at times the scenes from the Capitol hinted towards something stranger, something which resonated with our propositions. For a time, the events did not seem to quite fit with any one of the genres typically used to make sense of events. An attempted but always doomed insurrection, yes, but perhaps other things as well, expressing and eliciting other feelings: tourist visit, protest, occupation, riot, looting, opportunity for selfies, media spectacle intensified through retweets and evident enjoyment, and much more. Contributing to the strangeness of the event, were the scenes of excess which circulated afterwards: scenes of violence and of calls for violence typical of insurrection but mixed with placards pronouncing ever more outlandish conspiracy theories of baby eating and blood drinking, and featuring individuals dressed in outfits more absurd than politically resonant.

As we watched, we wondered and worried. Did this event lay bare what happens when the optimism of right-wing populism is threatened and an end, even if only temporary, looms for already violent fantasies (a more dramatic, dangerous end than the "fraying" or "waning" of fantasies that Berlant (2011) diagnoses)? The temporal loop optimism of right-wing populism is constitutionally fragile, always menaced by the cast of characters who stand opposed to a single, true "people". To "stop the steal" was to stop the return of forces responsible for a doomed present, for a betrayed world. To stop the return of the "common sense" of a multiracial liberalism or (worse yet?) the ascendancy of progressive censure. The feeling of having been robbed by enemies who supposedly stand outside and against "the people": this was the structure of feeling that "stop the steal" tapped into. What the people felt robbed of was evidently not merely Trump's presence in the White House but *a future* – one in which *their* wounds would be seen, their feelings recognised, their rightful agency affirmed. The desperate optimism of the insurrection was a gambit for recovery in the wake of this and other rapidly disappearing futures. As we watched the insurrectionists scaling the Capitol building – gawked at the impossibility of their mission, the outrageousness of the act, the capacity for violence – we also saw, crystallised in that moment, populism's structure of feeling: the empowering *affirmation* of the people (loved, sovereign), its performative *excess* (a costumed siege), and the *optimism* of its aim (a lost future restored).

Our aim in offering these three propositions has been to *feel our way into* the structure of feeling of right-wing populism. That is, we have sought to understand how right-wing populism in the US and the UK unfolds not as a set of commitments first and foremost (though there are certainly common aims) but as a characteristic way in which affective investments and attachments are organised and become available to people as resources for making sense of themselves, others, and their worlds. How populist feelings become available and attractive to some and not others, how they work to elevate certain subjects and their feelings and to denigrate others, percolates through these three propositions about what populism feels like. As we argue in the next two chapters, formations of progressivism and liberalism will organise attachments and investments differently, albeit with overlaps and resonances. They too will distribute not only intensity (that is, passion and excitement) but also disaffection and withdrawal – not as the exception but as part of what shores up the politics of feeling, allows it to take on the emergent consistencies of populism, progressivism, or liberalism today.

3
Progressivism: Redemptive, Catastrophic, and Intense

Introduction: Progressivism after the Future

> There is a voice in Margot's head. It says: You can't get there from here.
> She sees it all in that instant, the shape of the tree of power. Root to tip, branching and re-branching. Of course, the old tree still stands. There is only one way, and that is to blast it entirely to pieces. (Alderman, 2016: 364)

The passage is from Naomi Alderman's 2016 feminist speculative novel and *New York Times* bestseller, *The Power*. The moment comes late in the novel, as the story inches towards 'the Cataclysm': the final transfer of global power from men to women, achievable only, it turns out, by blasting the existing order 'entirely to pieces'. Alderman's vision is dark, for the Cataclysm inaugurates a world of (chromosomally defined) female power no better than the one it replaces; as one reviewer put it, the conclusion seems to be that 'the arc of the universe doesn't bend towards justice so much as inscribe a circle away from it' (El-Mohtar, 2017). Yet whatever one might feel about *The Power*'s dystopian conclusion, part of what makes it so unsettling is the familiarity of what propels this narrative: a feeling that we can't get *there* from *here*.

This, we argue, is the feeling that troubles progressivism's relationship to the future. To make progress is to advance, with effort, incrementally, towards some desirable end; to progress from *here* to *there*. There are various articulations of what end it is that progressives (across historical moments and diverse polities) are heading towards, but as scholars of politics and history have suggested, progressivism generally points towards a moral vision for a "good society", whatever that might be. Progressivism as an historical phenomenon does not embed a single vision of what the good is, only that it can be reached. In this sense, progressivism, like populism, is mobile and can be harnessed to a spectrum of political ideologies. With this lack of definitive content, progressivism falls short of being an ideology by conventional definition. Michael Freeden, the leading scholar of ideology studies, wrapped up his review of progressivism thus: 'We can state fairly conclusively that progressivism is not an ideology, but that being progressive is a disposition of some ideologies, telling us something about their temperament, their tempo, their values and their ambitions' (2014: 69).

Perhaps it is a quality of wispy structures of feeling – orientations such as populism or progressivism that don't quite congeal into fully fledged ideologies – to tell their entire story in their name. For just as populism takes its name from its distinctive agent (the *populi*), the substance of progressivism is on the semantic surface: progress, the principle or action of forward momentum itself. Just as populism is not the same as authoritarianism (though it may accompany this), progressivism is not equivalent to Marxism, communism, or socialism – all of which can be described as systems of ideas and *may* be progressive but also might lean towards a revolutionary politics or politics of rupture, rather than the feeling-structure of "progress". But how can "forward momentum" shape a distinctive structure of feeling? Isn't politics always a field of promises about the future? How can a disposition towards futurity itself distinguish any one political orientation? And how can progressivism have gathered force in a conjunctural crisis marked by the absence of the future?

Progressivism (like liberalism) is bound up with Western modernity's idea of its own political and moral trajectory: the Enlightenment confidence that whatever barbarism might lie in its past, the future of Europe (and by imperial extension, the world) would tend towards justice and peace (Kant, 1784 [1963]). In the context of Western modernity, since the 18th century, *progress* came to stand for the inevitable good that results from the right management of natural tendencies, which over time became inseparable from mythical notions of global capitalism and liberal democracy. Despite countervailing evidence and the ever-presence of critique, the assumptions of progressive secular development carried forward into subsequent incarnations of progressivism as a political label. As Emily Robinson puts it in *The Language of Progressive Thought in Modern Britain*, progressivism as it emerged in 20th-century Britain was based on 'an appeal to technocratic reasoning, in which good politics is simply a matter of managing the impersonal forces of change' (Robinson, 2017: 17).

From the perspective of the progressive left in the US and the UK today, this technocratic (liberal) promise is no longer convincing. The forces of change have become unhinged and managing them is no simple matter. The future whose wings are folded within the egg of the present is forecast to be monstrous: an increasingly uninhabitable earth, mass extinction and displacement, authoritarianism on the upswing, crumbling economies, infrastructures lurching past the point of repair, and fully militarised police enforcing the state-sanctioned dehumanisation of Black people, immigrants, LGBTQ+ people, women, the disabled, and the unhoused. It is not only that progressivism's end (the "good society") has fallen from the forecast, but that the very principle of progress itself – having played its historical role in justifying the West's destructive trajectory – has epistemically enabled the emergence of its own foul double: a present from which no good future emanates.

In the place of yesterday's techno-utopias, the futures that populate today's progressive imaginaries are catastrophic. Even the optimistic promise that "Another World is Possible" (a slogan originating in Latin American anti-corporate globalisation movements and gaining global currency in the 2000s; see McNally, 2006) raises the question of what we will do with *this* one. This is not to say that progressives are the only ones riveted to a threatening horizon. Coming catastrophes include not only climate change, authoritarianism, and capitalism's final feeding frenzy, but *The Coming Woke Catastrophe* (Heitzman, 2022), the coming pandemic catastrophe (worse than the last), nuclear Armageddon, and the ascendancy of artificial intelligence over humanity. Indeed, popular culture manifests an insatiable thirst for the apocalypse (causing it, preventing it, surviving it, living in its aftermath), in ways that amplify the generalised sense of precariousness we discussed in the introduction. Contortions of time and space in the affective field of the cataclysm include cinematic time-loops that stave off any future until we're ready and multiversal imaginaries that proliferate our options (Secor and Blum, 2023). But while forecasting and imagining 'end times' has become a widespread pursuit, the sense that our present moment is incubating a calamitous future presents a particular problem for progressivism as a structure of feeling that has historically had a positive relation to an unfolding future at its core. With climatic, environmental, and social collapse looming on the horizon, it is perhaps unsurprising that progressivism has been called an 'idea whose time has gone' (Blaazer, 2014).

And yet here it is again. At a time when the progressive optimism of Western modernity has largely gone off the rails, progressivism has re-emerged within political discourse. This re-emergence has included institutionalised and programmatic dimensions. In the US in 2022, the Congressional Progressive Caucus, which was founded in 1991 to represent the left-wing of the Democratic Party, won a record number of Democratic seats and became the largest Democratic caucus in the House of Representatives. In Britain in 2016 following the Brexit referendum, the left-leaning Labour Party pressure group, Compass, shifted its remit to advocate for a 'progressive alliance' that would bring Labour, Liberal Democrats, and Green Party constituencies together to defeat conservative forces; as the director of Compass wrote in *The Guardian*, 'If we want a red, green and liberal future we need to meld the politics of these essential strands into a coherent and consistent political project, with urgency because the march of national populism wants to strip democracy of its power to deliver the hope of this good society' (Lawson, 2021). The campaign for a progressive alliance disintegrated with the exit of the Green Party in 2023. But for a moment, *progressivism* had appeared as a quilting point for a coalition capable of countering the rise of populism in the name of 'the good society' to come.

Beyond the fluctuations of its fortunes in electoral politics in both countries, progressivism has become an increasingly popular label. Despite attempts (in Britain, in particular) to marry progressivism with centre-right politics (as exemplified by David Cameron's somewhat oxymoronic 'progressive conservativism'), in the 21st century progressivism's associations with left or centre-left politics have prevailed. In 2021 in the US, the Pew Research Center's study of political typology introduced a new category, indicating that 12 per cent of Democratic voters comprised the 'progressive left'. While occupying the far end of the liberal-democratic spectrum, and despite being the smallest segment of the coalition, progressives were notably the 'most politically active Democratic-oriented group' (Pew, 2021a; see also Pew, 2021b). They were also, in general, relatively young, highly educated, and more likely to be white (two-thirds) than any other group in the Democratic camp. In the UK as well, though lagging the US, the progressive label has taken on new meaning and salience since 2016. While a 2012 YouGov survey found that fewer than 5 per cent of respondents associated progressivism with the social justice left, by 2023 the term was in common circulation in the UK to refer to a left which is "woke" in the sense of cultivating and maintaining an alertness to injustice.

On the surface this is a bit of a puzzle: How has progressivism managed to resurge in the US and the UK *after* the presumption of inevitable progress associated with "modernity" has been gutted? In its earlier incarnations, progressivism positioned change as inevitable, reform as a matter of keeping up with the times. In today's incarnation, progressivism is generally located to the left of the "moderate" or "establishment" liberalism we focus on in the next chapter. For example, a *New York Times* piece in 2023 explained progressivism as in tension over the very question of incrementalism:

> Progressive is a label that encompasses various factions within the American left and can mean different things to different people. Broadly, progressives tend to believe the government should push for sweeping change to solve problems and address racial and social inequities. [...] [P]oints of tension emerge between moderates and progressives over tactics: Progressives tend to call for ambitious structural overhauls of U.S. laws and institutions that they see as fundamentally racist over incremental change and more measured policy approaches. (Ulloa and Lerer, 2023)

Favouring *sweeping* change and *ambitious* overhauls, progressivism today appears to be the impetuous version of liberalism. In this description, progressivism may share some of liberalism's professed goals ('to address racial and social inequalities'), but it is distinguished from liberalism by its unruly passion (its lack of *measure*) and its tendency towards 'ambitious structural overhauls'. This puts progressivism in the company of right-wing populism: differentiated from liberalism by its excessiveness. But while populists condemn liberal institutions for "elitism" or "globalism" (often implying that they are anti-nativist), for left progressives today, it is the historical entanglement of these institutions and laws with racist and colonial structures of power that renders them compromised and requires transformative action in the present.

The progressive call for action at the very site where the promise of progress might appear to have stalled out is well articulated in President Barack Obama's second inaugural speech on 21 January 2013. After four years in office mostly devoured by the post-2008 "Great Recession", Obama's speech seemed to promise a more social justice-oriented second term. Invoking 'Seneca Falls, and Selma, and Stonewall', and the 1963 March on Washington, Obama presented a vision of progress and a call for action:

It is now our generation's task to carry on what those pioneers began. For our journey is not complete until our wives, our mothers and daughters can earn a living equal to their efforts. Our journey is not complete until our gay brothers and sisters are treated like anyone else under the law [...] Our journey is not complete until no citizen is forced to wait for hours to exercise the right to vote. Our journey is not complete until we find a better way to welcome the striving, hopeful immigrants who still see America as a land of opportunity until bright young students and engineers are enlisted in our workforce rather than expelled from our country. [...] Being true to our founding documents does not require us to agree on every contour of life. It does not mean we all define liberty in exactly the same way or follow the same precise path to happiness. Progress does not compel us to settle centuries-long debates about the role of government for all time, but it does require us to act in our time. (Obama, 2013)

'Our generation' is enjoined to take up the incomplete journey, to finish what has somehow, until now, been impossible to complete. This is the specific and noble mission of the present: *It is now our generation's task*. But while the notion of completing a journey suggests taking the next step on a continuous path, in fact Obama's speech draws a line between disjointed points. Rather than marking out a trajectory, the events invoked (Selma, Stonewall, the March) are clustered within a few years of one another in the 1960s (with the 1848 Seneca Falls convention on women's rights having taken place in an entirely different era). The 'journey' constructed is an alternative line, one that directly feeds the momentous and historical triumphs of civil rights in the late 1960s into the present impasse. Progressivism thus repairs its timeline by patching together a past that waits to be fully redeemed with a heightened (no longer impassive) present tasked with rescuing the future.

Perhaps the loss of faith in progress that makes contemporary progressivism paradoxical is part of a larger pattern within the progressive structure of feeling: a pattern of withdrawal, of finding one's objects of attachment inadequate. Obama's second inaugural speech itself was greeted both with praise for its 'forceful argument for a progressive agenda' and scepticism about whether Obama himself would have the will or the wherewithal to carry it out (Editorial NYT, 2013). Indeed, many would dispute the notion that Obama *is* a progressive (rather than liberal) political figure. This is a broader characteristic of progressivism, in that unlike right-wing populism, it does not maintain consistent attachment to leaders. Even the revered icon of progressive politics, US Representative for New York Alexandria Ocasio-Cortez, regularly 'comes under fire for not being progressive enough' on issues such as Palestine or President Biden's candidacy for a second term – departures from progressive expectations that do not simply become part of a complex profile but recast her as an inadequate vessel for progressive aims (Fandos, 2024; Phillips, 2024). When it comes to political leaders, progressivism's 'purity politics' (in Alexis Shotwell's terms, 2016) undermines unconditional attachment and instead encourages the rooting out of inconsistency and compromise. For progressivism, there is an always present danger (even inevitability) of betrayal when it comes to political leaders or spokespeople.

What does it mean for progressivism to be strung out between hope and despair, between its promise and its own lost future? In the three propositions that follow, we focus on aspects of progressive culture and atmosphere (rather than primarily on progressive political figures) to critique the past, present, and future tense of progressive feeling. Our first proposition is that *for progressivism, while things are not good, they also haven't been better*. It is in this uncomfortable relationship to the past, we argue, that contemporary progressivism begins to differentiate from populist and liberal structures of feeling. The second proposition is that, with the shadow of apocalyptic politics falling over the promise of a "good society" to come, *progressivism is intensified by its own impasse*. This impasse, we argue, is not only the gap between the promise of progress and the catastrophic future that appears to lie in store but also a fissure within the progressive structure of feeling that elevates white affect and white political redemption by projecting the destruction that has already been accomplished onto the horizon. Finally, our third proposition addresses the present in which, we argue, *for progressives, everything matters now*. Everything is at stake in a present moment that has the capacity, in its intensity, both to eclipse the unredeemed wreckage of the past and to deflect the catastrophe threatening on the horizon. After the future, in the midst of intense precariousness and on the high seas of the digital mediated present, progressivism finds its intensity – and its exhaustion – in the urgency of preventing the arrival of the worse-yet.

Proposition 1: For Progressivism, While Things Are Not Good, They Also Haven't Been Better

That the present is disastrous and in need of repair has long been the starting point for progressive politics (Nugent, 2009). Today, the signs are everywhere and inescapable. Seen, felt, and understood from the perspective of social justice, the present is little but an accumulation of connected disasters. Melting glaciers, homeless encampments, rising food bank use, heatwaves, a vicious anti-trans atmosphere, police violence, and endemic anti-blackness: the list is ever expanding. The signs are everywhere and inescapable. Alongside and underneath these visible signs of existing dystopias are fast and slow violences that deplete, constrain, and damage people's lives. Environmental harm, the displacements of gentrification, endemic hunger, structural precarity, stress, and burnout are among the effects of the speeded-up circulations of capital. Too often below the threshold of public awareness and action, their revelation by activists and others adds to the sense of the present as an unfolding dystopia.

"Crisis" becomes the predominant, alarm-imbued feeling of the present. Not unique to progressives, crisis nevertheless serves as a shared way of naming and feeling a damaged, ruinous present, in which the worst could still be to come, but the present is unquestionably a mess. Whatever progressives are concerned with, from housing to climate change, racial injustice to sanitation, the shared feeling is of both present harm and imminent collapse. As Rheinhart Koselleck (2006) shows, the concept of *crisis* has long been put to work in relation to different kinds of events and situations. But in the overheated present, "crisis" is no longer easily set against a non-crisis normality. Crisis is permanent and continuous, rather than a rupture, temporary or exceptional. The "normal" is no longer available as a site of comfort that can be returned to and unproblematically (re)attached to once an aberrant crisis is resolved. Rather than returning from the condition of crisis to a baseline normality, as we saw amid COVID-19, calls proliferate for a "new normal" that would overcome the disaster that is the present. Climate change exemplifies the collapsing line between exceptional crisis and stable normality. Normality cannot be returned to "after" the climate crisis has somehow been concluded because normality itself, in the sense of fossil fuel intensive modes of living and attachments, is the grounds for the perpetual crisis.

Affirmation of such a disastrous present is both impossible and obscene. But salvation cannot be found by returning to a better past. Our first proposition is that *for progressivism, while things are not good, they also haven't been better.* For the past was just as bad, or worse – especially for women, Black and brown people, and LGBTQ+ people. Moreover, the violence and injustices of the past – such as colonialism, slavery, and fossil fuel use – have brought us to our current crisis. There is no good, available past to be returned to. If it appears that there might be, this is simply because the violence and injustice of the era has yet to be revealed and reckoned with. Every epoch was marked by injustices or created new ones that quickly overshadowed any apparent progress, which was always denied or delayed. Every past time can become, retrospectively, a scene of injustice to be revealed. Understood in this way, "the past" cannot serve as an unproblematic object of attachment, in the way that it must do, albeit in different ways, for both right-wing populism and liberalism.

Take, for example, the difficulty of nostalgia for the crumbling and now ended "post-war settlement" as some kind of pre-neoliberal golden age of prosperity. Residual elements of the post-World War II settlement are present in parts of progressive left culture, especially when security is invoked by politicians as a promise in contrast with today's precarity. For example, a campaign video for Jeremy Corbyn from 2018 promises to rebuild Britain, against a background of multiple losses: 'We lost the factories, we lost the jobs, we lost confidence in our community, we lost control', the advert begins (Corbyn, 2018). The promise was of change in the form of 'kickstarting the economy in all the regions of the country, so our economy works for everyone'. Central to the hope of growth without inequality was the return of a residual Fordist promise of security and dignity through work: that investment would create 'good jobs, with decent wages, not short-term insecure work, but good jobs for the long term'. However, while it is possible to harken back to the post-war settlement as a point when the social contract was stronger, and inequality less stark in the US and the UK, or when liberal tenets were more broadly accepted, it cannot serve as an unproblematic "good" from the perspective of *social justice*, despite the continued attachment to the security it offered to some and is invoked by the Labour Party advert. It is now difficult to name or invoke the post-war settlement without, at the same time, emphasising how it was built on the back of repressive gender roles and relations organised around the nuclear family, forms of anti-blackness, and the continuation of debilitating forms of work that wore out the bodies of people attached to the affective bargains of Fordism. Just as affirmation of the present is both impossible and obscene, so too is any nostalgic relation with the past. To be nostalgic is to forget the bad that the past was, or, worse, to be complicit in it.

Is detachment from the past new to today's progressives? Progressive time cannot, by definition, be founded on the promise of a return to a better past. It typically involves the assumption of a movement towards an ever better but never finished, never perfected, future, even if that movement might be bumpy or interrupted. As Obama put it multiple times during his presidential terms, reworking the words of Martin Luther King Jr, himself borrowing from the abolitionist Theodore Parker: 'the arc of the moral universe is long, but it bends toward justice'.[1] Consequently, the past cannot be unproblematically attached to because things can always be, will always be, better in the future. Perhaps, then, a rejection of the past is a constitutive part of all progressive movements?

But we think there is something different at work in progressivism today. Progressive time involves a weak attachment

---

[1] Parker's original quote contains far more hesitancy, and little of the determination that has come to be associated with the phrase: 'I cannot pretend to understand the moral universe; the arc is a long one, my eye reaches but little ways; I cannot calculate the curve and complete the figure by the experience of sight; I can divine it by conscience. And from what I see I am sure it bends toward justice' (Theodore Parker, 1853, cited in Ratcliffe, 2017, n.p.).

to the past alongside a constitutive *detachment*. The past must be detached from, as it is what progress has left behind. And yet, in a traditional understanding of progress, there remains a weak attachment to the past as a steady journey of improvement, each era better than the one that preceded it: a perpetual, albeit bumpy, movement forward. It is this assumption of linear, continuous, improvement that is fraying in the midst of a precarious present and after the loss of the future. It is no longer that easy to attach to the historical determinism lurking in Obama's use of versions of a phrase commonly attributed to Martin Luther King Jr. What is lost is a past-present relation that can be attached to as evidence of the continuous movement of improvement. Or, put differently, what is lost to progressives today is a weak attachment to an imperfect past, one that nevertheless served as evidence for the continuous movement of progress.

We wonder whether today the progressive relation with the past is best captured by Walter Benjamin's famous and much commented upon angel of history, who, on looking back, witnesses only an accumulation of disasters:

A Klee painting named "Angelus Novus" shows an angel looking as though he is about to move away from something he is fixedly contemplating. His eyes are staring, his mouth is open, his wings are spread. This is how one pictures the angel of history. His face is turned toward the past. Where we perceive a chain of events, he sees one single catastrophe which keeps piling wreckage upon wreckage and hurls it in front of his feet. The angel would like to stay, awaken the dead and make whole what has been smashed. But a storm is blowing from Paradise; it has got caught in his wings with such violence that the angel can no longer close them. This storm irresistibly propels him into the future to which his back is turned, while the pile of debris before him grows skyward. This storm is what we call progress. (Benjamin, 1968: 257–258)

The angel's mouth is open, perhaps in horror, perhaps in shock, perhaps in fascination, as they witness the wreckage that piles up before them. Carried forward by the storm of "progress", ever more wreckage piles up as past injustices are constantly revealed and newly reckoned with (and this revelation and reckoning with pasts becomes a site of contestation with right-wing populists, as we saw in the previous chapter, for whom the not-quite lost past can only ever be good).

However, this image of an angel stunned by the past and propelled by progress is not quite fitting to the progressive structure of feeling in the US and the UK today. This is because, as we shall see, what *really* horrifies and fascinates progressives today, what they turn to and cannot look away from, is not the wreckage of the past but a future full of catastrophes. And unlike for Benjamin and Klee's angel, the past is not wholly lost for today's progressivists. The relation to the past is not simply a nihilistic one based only on negating the catastrophes that founded western modernity and its racial hierarchies and forms of destruction and dispossession. Here, we find a distinction with some forms of Black and Indigenous studies work and activism. The progressive bad past is not a complete, world-founding and world-ending catastrophe. It is not the catastrophe that has already happened, the abyss of anti-blackness that modernity and progressive time rests upon (Warren, 2018). Yes, the past was bad, but hope remains. Amid the wreckage that continues to pile up and hold progressives' horrified and fascinated gaze, are fragments that serve to keep the possibility that things might be different and better alive. Fragments of the "almost good past" can be found everywhere, across diverse peoples, periods, and places who have claimed and enacted justice. These past futures are diverse, housed in the re-occurring figures (Martin Luther King Jr, Nelson Mandela), events (May 1968, civil rights marches, Stonewall riots), institutions ("the NHS"), and movements (Act Up, the suffragettes) that progressives bring into the present and honour. They might be the 'freedom dreams' that Robin Kelly (2002) gathers and documents, examples of actually existing utopias, or pre-figurative moments. They might be already existing elements of public culture that offer longstanding scenes of attachment for people to attach to, or they might be hidden, silenced, or suppressed peoples that need to be given voice, recognised and celebrated.

Consider, for example, the presence of the 1984–1985 miners' strike in UK progressive left culture. The events have long exercised a fascination in British culture. Part of a longstanding class-based fascination with the heroic, masculine "real" labour of miners (e.g. Orwell, 1937), the events have served to mark a turning point in British culture that helps explain the present.[2] In left culture, the strike is an occasion of tragic defeat – a continued visceral wound that serves as the occasion of Thatcher's triumph, the defeat of organised labour by the authoritarian state, and the devastation of working class northern and Midlands communities. While signifying all this and the culmination of a shift between political–economic settlements, the miners' strike is also remembered and made present as something more. The strike lives on as an exemplar of intense solidarity but also, as David Nettleingham (2017: 855)

---

[2] For recent examples of the representations of the miners' strike associated with the forty-year anniversary, see documentaries *Miners' Strike: A Frontline Story* (BBC, 2024) and *Miners' Strike 1984: The Battle for Britain* (Channel 4, 2024), as well as recent dramatisations that focus on the aftermath of defeat, and associated affects of abandonment, shame–pride, and resentment, like *Sherwood* (BBC, 2022) and *The Way* (BBC, 2024).

argues, as 'the fork where two alternative futures divert; one in which working-class people have greater power, the other where working-class communities are devastated'. And as well as place-based class solidarities, recent histories and dramatisations of the strike makes it into an occasion for new reciprocal solidarities across differences of class, race, gender, and sexuality (Kelliner, 2015). A fragment of a good past exists even amid historic defeat. Another future was possible, even if the actual future turned out to be a disaster made from the fast violences of the authoritarian state and the slow violences of abandonment.

Because of the presence of fragments of the good past, the past (and present) need not be wholly negated, despite the harms that pile up in the present. As with the 1984–1985 miners' strike, fragments of good pasts offer resources for progressives to attach to, without contradicting the claim that the past was bad and should not be returned to. They act in the present as evidence that something different and better did or almost happened, even if the justice they called for or enacted was ultimately denied or deferred. Hence the flurry of interest, engagement, and attachment to alternative, revisionist histories that re-centre marginalised subjects and peoples left out of the historical record (e.g. the 1619 project, Hannah-Jones, 2024). Past events, figures, and movements exist in the present as partial, incomplete, or thwarted "wins", sometimes examples of justice enacted, but as often justice denied, deferred, ended, or perverted. Irrespective of whether they tragically or heroically failed or spawned their own disasters, they can be attached to as evidence that things might have been otherwise, evidence that the bad present was never inevitable. By being brought into the present, they become "past futures" – examples that keep the hope alive that other presents than this disaster could have happened.

Fragments of the past solve the problem of hope for progressives. If the evidence of the crisis-present and bad past means that hope in the straight time of progress is no longer possible, hope can still be found in the paths began but not taken, the forks in the road, the interruptions, and detours. Amid the pile-up of disasters, hope remains by returning and celebrating the abundant fragments of almost-justice that are littered throughout history. This is not the past to be preserved in the present, and certainly not returned to, nor is it the imperfect past embedded in continuous, linear time. Rather, they are pasts to be recognised and honoured because they confirm, again and again, the weak hope that has served as the counterpoint to the pessimistic realism of "there is no alternative" and is expressed in the slogan and affirmation: "Another world is possible".

The result is the curious and counterintuitive founding of progressivism today on a form of non-linear rather than linear time, albeit a time that cannot be returned to. For the past contains ruptures and interruptions, forks in the road that just about sustain the conviction that there *were* alternatives, and perhaps therefore still are. Perhaps the solidarity across differences of the eighty-four to eighty-five miners' strike can be rekindled? Perhaps the energies of the Stonewall riots or the civil rights movement can once again propel progressive politics in a time of anti-trans or anti-Black violence? But the promise is weak, because every "past future" that is attached to was, fundamentally, a failure because of how the crisis present has turned out. Progressive hope today can only be a weak hope, ever shrouded in past disappointment and touched by evidence of past failure in today's crisis time. It's a weak hope that, as we shall see, must face a future that appears ever more hopeless.

Proposition 2: Progressivism Is Intensified by Its Own Impasse

Pervasive as it is, "apocalyptic politics" is an inherent impasse for progressivism. Projecting a bad future unfolding from the (bad) present (which itself follows from the mounting wreckage of the bad past) subverts the idea of progress and of progressive thought – perhaps even inverts it, creating an "upside down" of progressivism in its place. Our proposition is that this paradox is not incidental to the affective structure of progressivism today but, in fact, is the fission that fuels it. This is the affective charge that circulates between the anti-capitalist mantra, "Another world is possible", and the slogan "There is no plan(et) B" that originated in climate activism in Britain (coined by comedian–activist Robert Newman, see Logan, 2006). At the same time as progressivism attaches to the (hopeful) possibility of *another world*, it raises the question of the relationship between this other (good) world and the one that we currently inhabit, the one that seems to be spinning towards a catastrophic horizon. This conundrum is at once an impasse and an engine. It generates progressive affect not only through the dynamics of anticipatory action that, by situating the present forever on the precipice of disaster, perpetuate the urgency of present action (Anderson, 2010), but more specifically by projecting images of the catastrophic past onto an apocalyptic future – a move that we will argue ultimately elevates and recuperates whiteness within the structure of feeling. In short, progressivism generates potency through its own reversals, splittings, and differentiation.

Invested in the idea that a bad future is incubating in our (already not good) present, progressivism today appears to be a structure of feeling at odds with its own basic premise. Perhaps counterintuitively, this is evident explicitly in the expression of progressive hope that attached early on to the COVID-19 pandemic. In 2020–2021 in the US and the UK, the shock of lockdowns and the accompanying global recession became fuel for progressive hope that "another world" might yet emerge from this one. With tourism and other travel constrained and shops and schools closed (at different times and to different degrees in different places), "nature is healing" became a popular meme, featuring (often misleading) images of wild animals in urban environments (Bosworth, 2022). The surge of worker resignations that followed the reopening of workplaces and the end of state-sponsored furloughs and other stop-gap measures was deemed the "Great Resignation" and taken to signify a collective rejection of exploitative working conditions. This, like the "return" of swans to Venice (whence they had never left) proved illusory, more a continuation of workforce trends than the dawning of a new era (Secor et al., 2024). Yet in the spirit of such hope for a crisis-opportunity, an influential 2021 article on "post-pandemic transformations" in *World Development* concludes:

> While recognising the failures to learn lessons from past disease outbreaks where similar themes have emerged, we strike a note of optimism. The scale and depth of the COVID-19 crisis, and its North-South universality, perhaps mean that, this time, progressive transformations will emerge – in different places, in different ways – that embrace uncertainty, unruliness and inevitable complexity, while equally confronting the structures of mainstream capitalist development that give rise to persistent crises, generate unequal vulnerabilities and impede progressive change. Of course, power and politics will intervene, incumbent interests will naturally resist and opportunists may fill the vacuum, but the required changes are in the end political choices, requiring democratic struggle and mobilisation. If such far-reaching transformative change does not emerge, the project of

'development' will have failed, and future shocks – for they will surely come – will wreak even greater havoc. (Leach et al., 2021: 138)

There is a fork in the road, a branch in the timeline. In one scenario, the global pandemic-crisis shakes loose existing blockages to progressive change and thereby puts progressive time back on track. In the other, this does not happen and therefore "development" itself (scare quotes and all) will have failed, seeding a still greater catastrophe in the future. It is this latter scenario, marked by the failure of the old frameworks of incremental improvement (whether development or progress) and the threat of *even greater havoc* in the wake of this failure, that is most salient to progressive feeling today in the US and the UK. And indeed, despite the cautious optimism of some progressives in the early period of the pandemic, the shadow of catastrophes to come (the spectre of mass disablement, a brewing civil war in the US, and disaster capitalism in the UK) lay heavily over the season. In the end, the pandemic seemed to fuel conspiracy theories, enrich billionaires, and worsen the NHS and state schools in Britain, rather than bring about progressive change. Even this guarded hope placed in crisis-opportunity is disappointed.

This sense that a bad future, one marked by progressivism's failure, is unfolding from our troubled present is not an aberration of progressive affect or a bleed across its boundaries (a tip towards a politics of rupture). Instead, it is this apparent perversity of progressivism today that orients and abrades progressivism's structure of feeling in the current conjuncture. Responses to the climate crisis exemplify the progressive orientation towards the future as the "worse to come" on the heels of a barbarous past. Given that the past discovery, extraction, and use of fossil fuels is responsible for today's ecological degradation, there is no good past available to unambivalently return to (other than perhaps an impossible-to-recover, romanticised, image of a pre-modern indigenous past of harmonious human and non-human coexistence). While the history of Western civilisation can only be encountered and related to as the start of the disaster, one which continues to have harmful legacies today through the accumulation of toxic materialities, the climate-changed future threatens to be worse still. Climate-changed futures are made present through the images and atmospheres of catastrophe: the frequent recourse to vocabularies of extinction and the end of all possible worlds. Unfolding in the disastrous present of increasing extreme events, the "worse to come" threatens a future shorn of any possible redemption in a past powered by fossil fuels (Folkers, 2021). As Amy Robson (2024) convincingly argues, the time of climate catastrophe shifts the loss of this world and ways of life founded on whiteness from the past of worlds-destroying indigenous dispossession to the future where a new catastrophe brews.

Situating politics in the shadow of the coming catastrophe is how progressivism recovers from the discomfort of the "bad past", invests the present with political significance, and *elevates white affective orientations* within progressive futurity. This elevation occurs even though progressivism's impasse, its loss of tempo, is intimate with what Rizvanna Bradley calls 'the stalled temporality of waiting so distinctive to black life': a time of 'suspended action' at 'the nexus of stolen pasts, of protracted presents without presence, of futurities withheld' (Bradley, 2023: 205). For at the same time as it grapples with the "temporality without duration' that Bradley discusses, progressive politics *re-intensifies* the present in a way that departs from this impassivity. By turning its impasse into the site of passionate intensity, progressivism arguably subsumes what Tyrone Palmer (2017: 32) calls the 'opacity and *unthinkability* of Black feeling', while at the same time inscribing it at the heart of the progressive present.

For if what is at stake in the present moment is the destruction of the world, our times are filled with urgent purpose. And if the worst is still on the horizon, then it hasn't already been accomplished. And if you think the worst hasn't happened, maybe it just hasn't happened *to you*. In this sense, progressivism engages in what Elizabeth Povinelli calls 'the repetition compulsion of late liberalism, whereby the different toxic accumulations of racial and colonial catastrophes are refigured as a coming catastrophe for humanity' (2021: 16, emphasis in the original; see also Hartman, 2002). The projection of the worst into the future (the 'even greater havoc' of which Leach et al., 2021, warn) acts as a shield against the horror of what has already happened, the irreversibility of damage upon which the present moment rests.

Another example of how progressivism's catastrophic horizons rely on white detachment from historical catastrophes can be traced in how Margaret Atwood's 1985 novel *The Handmaid's Tale* and its television adaptation have been taken up in political discourse, especially in the US. From 2017, the red cloak and blinkering white bonnet that the Hulu series made iconic began to appear at pro-choice protests, most prominently in the US but also in the UK, Ireland, Argentina, and elsewhere. In 2019, *Wired* magazine called it the 'viral protest uniform of 2019', a new symbol of dissent to rival the Guy Fawkes mask in its visuality and vagueness (Ellis, 2019). In May 2022, when a leak revealed that the Supreme Court was set to overturn Roe v. Wade (the decision that had protected the right to abortion in the US), *The Atlantic* published an article penned by Atwood herself. The headline read, 'I invented Gilead. The Supreme Court is making it real,' with the subtitle hammering home the point: 'I thought I was writing fiction in *The Handmaid's Tale*' (Atwood, 2022).

Many have dissected the politics of race, class, gender, and liberalism perpetuated by both Atwood's book and the show that followed (e.g. Holladay and Classen, 2021; Neville-Shepard, 2023). In the context of our effort to understand the role that catastrophic futures such as Gilead play in the affective structure of progressivism, what is especially relevant is the critique that has ensued not only of Atwood's novel and the Hulu show itself but of the 'progressive fans of *The Handmaid's Tale*' who became iconic of a certain modality of gendered and raced progressive protest (Lewis, 2017). What made the 'handmaid' so compelling as a progressive icon and ultimately so controversial?

In part, it was a matter of timing. Based on Atwood's (1985) perennially read novel but going beyond its narrative arc, *The Handmaid's Tale* television series (created for Hulu by Bruce Miller) initially aired in April 2017, shortly after Trump's inauguration. The premise of both the novel and the series is that the country of Gilead has emerged from the overthrow of the United States by a Christian-fundamentalist group. In a world where fertility has inexplicably dropped, children have been redistributed to the wealthy and women who have proven able to give birth are enslaved and forced to bear children for their overlords. With scenes of US refugees amassing across Canada's border, the show immediately resonated with viewers alienated and frightened by Trump's 2016 election. Successive seasons, all of them bleak and tortuous, secured *The Handmaid's Tale*'s role as dystopian fantasy for times of high political anxiety. Gilead articulated a future at once fantastical and imminent. In a feedback loop of retroactive confirmation, unfolding events such as the repeal of Roe v. Wade in June 2022 seemed to confirm that Gilead was more than speculative.

The rise of the handmaid as a "woman's rights" icon did not sit well with everyone. As Sophie Lewis scathingly puts it, what progressives had latched onto was nothing but 'a deraced slave narrative about forced surrogacy (or reproductive ownership) on the American plantation, appropriated for the purposes of white feminist futurism' (Lewis, 2017). At the heart of the complaint against this activation of Gilead as a spectre of the bad future is the contention that what Atwood projects as a future dystopia had, in fact, already occurred. Enslavement, rape, forced sterilisation, and children being stolen by the state is not something located in a fantastical future. Rather, it is at once past and ongoing for Black and Indigenous people. Not only were such horrors visited in the past upon those forced into slavery and subjugated by settlers, but they are also presently repeated when children are forcibly separated from parents at the US–Mexican border, refugees are imprisoned or allowed to drown, and crimes against Black women go unpunished (see Avalos, 2023; Gorrie, 2018). By projecting the traumas of rape and reproductive enslavement onto the future and shifting it to white women, Gilead appears as a catastrophe that must (and can) be prevented (by an educated, progressive white woman who has lots of Black friends, if we take our cues from the Hulu show).

Setting the cataclysm in the future restores the possibility of white (largely middle-class) progressive mastery by suggesting that there is still an opportunity to avert *the worst* – and "we" are the ones to do it. This is a defence that psychoanalyst Donald Winnicott (1974) calls "annihilation anxiety": by moving the experience of loss and destruction from the past to the future, psychically speaking the prevention of the catastrophe becomes possible. Povinelli (2021: 37–38) describes the scene of such wilful ignorance as such: 'If you are sitting in certain places in Europe, the United States, and Australia, you will see a multitude of the middle class and affluent staring at the horizon [...] Already the effects are all around them [...] Yet still they stare at the horizon as if they will see the coming catastrophe or a savior standing there.'

There is in this a kind of "kettle logic" – an excess of defence – in the projection of the worst of the past onto the future. The *logique du chaudron* (as Jacques Derrida [1998] named it) derives from a story that Sigmund Freud (1953 [1900]) told in the context of dream analysis to describe how the dream-work obscures what the subject wishes not to confront. The story is of a man who accuses his neighbour of returning a borrowed kettle damaged, to which the neighbour objects, incoherently, that he returned the kettle undamaged, that the kettle was already damaged when he borrowed it, and that furthermore he never borrowed the kettle in the first place. Placing the catastrophe on the horizon of progressive politics similarly fans out an array of contradictory defences. On the one hand, apocalyptic politics gives white, privileged actors an opportunity to be "on the right side of history" and fight the very forces that have produced the impassive present. At the same time, it denies the cataclysmic, world-destroying violence of the past by suggesting it was "not the end of the world", since what counts as "the end" is yet to come (Colebrook, 2023). And while denying that the worst has already been accomplished, it yokes its political intensity to the urgency of preventing this world-ending violence (that has already been visited upon subjugated "others") from befalling (hitherto) privileged subjects in the future. This mirroring is also evident on the right; as Naomi Klein speculates, conspiracy theorists' fear of 'being rounded up, treated as second-class, occupied, and culled' may be because 'on some level they know that these are the genocidal behaviors that created and sustain their relative but increasingly precarious privilege' (Klein, 2023: 276). In other words, what this structure of feeling holds together is a series of defences that allow relatively affluent, white progressive subjects of the present to deflect "the worst" from the past to the future, to make "the worst" the destruction of their (our) own world, and thereby to affirm that they (we) certainly could never be (never have been) complicit in the world-destroying violence that has already happened. In the logic of the borrowed kettle, the competing denials of damage done deflect responsibility; their contradictions are no detriment to their aim.

Relying on white detachment from the historical catastrophes of chattel slavery, indigenous genocides, and colonialism – and on a denial of how what is supposed to be in the future is already present – progressivism (like populism) offers a balm for white uncertainty and anxiety. Yet at the same time, the political action and imagination of Black and other non-white progressives generate much of progressivism's affective magnetism. The centrality of Black Lives Matter, the high profile of Black, Latina/o and other non-white leaders in progressive politics, and even the adoption of the term "woke", which originated as a Black American colloquialism, all speak to the importance of anti-racism and Black and other racial and ethnic minorities' political mobilisation to progressivism today. The dominant whiteness of progressive affect is thus in tension with the constitutive and energetic importance of its antiracist and decolonial orientations that are key to how progressivism manages to recuperate the failures of past action and invest the present moment with urgent significance.

Proposition 3: Everything Matters Now

On Sunday, 27 March 2022, at the 94th Academy Awards at the Dolby Theatre in Los Angeles, presenter Chris Rock made a joke about Jada Pinkett Smith's shaved head and her husband,

Will Smith, came up on stage and slapped him across the face. Back in his seat, Smith yelled, 'Keep my wife's name out of your fucking mouth!'[3]

The scene went viral, sparking a Twitter storm and occupying prime billing on television talk shows, radio podcasts, and online news sources.[4] Reactions and "takes" proliferated, while interviews with celebrities, comedians, pundits, and experts added fresh material for further circulation and reaction. The sheer level of attention to this "unscripted" moment at the Academy Awards was itself a phenomenon worthy of note, earning it the wry distinction of "the slap felt round the world". The tongue-in-cheek reference to "the shot heard round the world" (that launched the American Revolutionary War in 1775 at the battles of Lexington and Concord) toys with the triviality of the celebrity dust-up and the staginess of the violence. And "around the world" might be a bit of an exaggeration; a Google Trends "incident" mapping reveals regions of greater (North America, Western Europe, Australia, New Zealand, South Africa) and lesser (South America, Russia, Eastern Europe) reverberation. But regardless, the analogy to the shot heard round the world (and the degree to which the incident was indeed a top-trending topic internationally) makes the point that – while other eras had their own significant events – here,

---

[3] Video of moment can be accessed here: www.youtube.com/watch?v=myjEoDypUD8&themeRefresh=1

[4] Despite claims to world-wide importance, the event was deemed most relevant in the US, though it did receive global coverage. And in fact, by 1 April 2022, the scene had gone from viral photo to meme to a mural on the Berlin Wall (see www.thenationalnews.com/arts-culture/art/2022/04/01/mural-of-will-smith-slapping-chris-rock-appears-in-berlin/).

now, today, *this* is what matters. Indeed, the revolutionary shot may have been *heard*, and it may have transmitted a message, but the slap was *felt*.

It was immediately understood that much was at stake in this altercation. But what exactly? Alopecia awareness, the physical safety of comedians, the excesses of "cancel culture", the future of the Academy Awards, the racism that Black men (no matter how famous) contend with, the agency of Black women? Was Smith 'showing up for his wife, and thus showing up more broadly for Black women' – something that Black men have been criticised for not doing (Neal, 2022)? Or was it a display of 'toxic masculinity' that 'spoke to the emotional limits of Will Smith, and then more broadly Black men, to not be able to show ways of support for Black women without going back to the old adage of using their hands, of force, of violence' (Neal, 2022)? Or then again, was the slap *in no way* supportive of Black women but rather an act that undermined Black women's agency, that even 'undid the work of Beyoncé's opening performance because it shoved a woman out of the center of her own story and replaced her experience with his violence' (Harris-Perry, 2022)? These are just a selection of the many ways, in the immediate aftermath, that the slap seemed to *matter*.

And while the public wrestled with whether (and in what tone) to condemn the slap, there was also the question of the joke itself. Was the joke a gentle ribbing, and the slap an 'overreaction' typical of 'cancel culture', the outsized power of women, and an ongoing 'war on jokes' (Maher, 2022)? Or was the joke itself far from innocent? If Rock did not know or suspect that Pinkett Smith's bald head was a sign of alopecia (something about which she had spoken openly, and which is not uncommon among Black women), 'This lack of knowledge of the kinds of chronic diseases that afflict Black women are

[sic] a form of toxic masculinity in and of itself' (Neal, 2022). What the proliferating reactions (including the official apologies and sanctions) had in common was that they granted the event – and, crucially, the *responses to the event* – the power to rectify, reveal, or retrench virtually *everything* that plagues the taut time of the (American) present. The unscripted moment was conscripted for a staged battle.

Everything is amplified, quickened, and sharpened in the digital mediated present. It is a time of high drama. The slap is just one example of an event that cannot be called trivial – or rather, calling it trivial itself carries the weight of an untrivial statement, demonstrating a detachment that itself matters and has effects. Everything is at stake, not simply in the event but in the *right response* to it. To get something wrong is consequential, a sign of *being* wrong (Levin and Bowker, 2019). The right response belongs to the righteous. The progressive present is therefore melodramatic, adhering to the conventions of 'a genre form that portrays dramatic events through moral polarities of good and evil, overwhelmed victims, heightened affects of pain and suffering, grand gestures, astonishing feats of heroism, and the redemption of virtue' (Anker, 2014: 2).

This melodramatic register is not unique to progressivism, but it does take on a unique form. As Elisabeth R. Anker (2014) argues, both conservative and left politics make use of the melodramatic genre to confer moral clarity on a world of intertwined (destructive) forces. In pitched battles between good and evil, it is possible to clearly identify perpetrators, victims, and the heroic agents of virtuous action. In a parallel to Anker's analysis of conservative melodrama, which reaffirms the state's sovereign power, we suggest that progressive melodrama reinstates the sovereignty of the subject as both a moral and political agent. Reframing the political arena as a moral realm, progressive melodrama pivots on questions of personal responsibility, guilt, reparation, and punishment. This moral drama is driven by an appeal to justice: to restore what has been lost and envision a more just future (Levine and Bowker, 2019). Along with projecting past catastrophe into the future, elevating the significance of right action and reaction in the present amplifies the political agency of the individual, the (potentially global) significance of their actions and reactions.

In the impasse between past and future catastrophes, progressivism takes on melodramatic tones to invest a 'fantasy of right feeling, politics, and action' (Yao, 2021: 210). Right action ensures that we will be able to "get there from here" and recuperate a lost continuity after the end of progressive History. In this sense, progressivism is hopeful: hopeful that there is something we can do to make things right, that the promise of progress is not lost. If *everything matters now*, there is always something we can do. Further, there is always something we *must* do because silence, inaction, or lack of awareness are the same as active perpetration of the worst. And if silence or a wrong "take" have the capacity to destroy and oppress, then *the right action now*, no matter how individual or fleeting, must have the power to set progressive time back on track. In the real-time of progressivism, there is no uniquely empowered actor or site of action, but rather, everything is at stake in everything for everyone. This conviction that *everything matters now* might be considered symptomatic of progressivism's "weak ideology", contrasting most dramatically, for example, with the (economistic) Marxist position that it is only by striking at the base of the system (the capitalist mode of production) that real progress can be made. Instead, progressivism in the present elevates the significance of what might appear incidental in the *this here now*. It is this political–affective saturation of the present moment that demonstrates progressivism as a structure of feeling: a 'developing form' that corresponds to nothing more than its own active, living, emergent edge (Williams, 1977: 129).

The high drama of *everything matters now* is expressed in the vocabulary and atmosphere of emergency that alongside crisis has become so central to narrating and feeling the precarious present and is used with increased frequency in relation to the climate crisis. Declaring that the present is an emergency is an act of hope. It implies that something can still be done to avert the worse to come, even if the time to act is fast running out. Now unmoored from the founding distinction between the exceptional and the normal, given the normalisation of precariousness we discussed in the introduction, emergency serves to charge the present with heightened, intense significance. Declarations and claims of an "unprecedented global climate emergency", for example, are partly issued in relation to climate impacts unfolding in a present now too full of "extreme events" and environmental degradations. But they gain their power from the claim that the future will be worse, potentially much worse – yet time remains. As Greta Thunberg put it in her speech to Devos in 2019:

Adults keep saying: "We owe it to the young people to give them hope". But I don't want your hope. I don't want to be hopeful. I want you to panic. I want you to feel the fear I feel every day. And then I want you to act.

I want you to act as you would in a crisis. I want you to act as if our house is on fire. Because it is. (Thunberg, 2019)

Infused with feelings of urgency, emergency and crisis blur as ways of maintaining the fragile hope that action in the present can still make a difference, that the worst future can be averted, that there can be a fork in the road or a branch in the timelines. Hope might not be felt, might even by rejected as per

Thunberg's words, but it is not extinguished if urgent action happens *right now*.[5] As the title of a collection on climate change and possibility edited by Rebecca Solnit and Thelma Lutunatabua (2023) stresses, it is "Not Too late". It is late, just not *too* late. The progressive gaze turns from the catastrophe to come to a present in which redemption for the past is still possible, even if the idea of ending the climate crisis, declaring the climate emergency over, might perhaps feel a little too optimistic.

When the appeal to justice fails to generate forward momentum, the progressive present becomes hyperbolic, provocative, repetitive, and self-devouring. Under these conditions, the intensification of a present in which *everything matters now* reverses back on itself, and the differentiation of progressive feeling once again unstitches its structure from within. For indeed much of the drama that unfolds in the progressive present is fuelled by white annihilation anxiety, convulsions of white guilt and shame, and attempts to restore (white) political agency in the face of the collapse of progressive teleology. With climate anxiety appearing as one

---

[5] Some climate activists in the bleed where liberal and progressive structures of feeling become indistinct have attempted to foster feelings of hope, or rather an attachment to its possibility (see Solnit and Lutunatabua, 2023). The wager is that hope is necessary to initiate and motivate present action or, put differently, that a relation with a good climate changed future is a pre-condition for intense action in the present. Often this hope is founded in fragments found in the otherwise disastrous present, hopeful stories that serve as anticipatory evidence that a different future composed of other human-non-human or human-environment relations is possible.

of the gathered strands of progressive feeling, it too has been critiqued for its whiteness, its imbrication with white fears of racialised migrant others ('It's a surprisingly short step from [...] ecoanxiety, to xenophobia and fascism' [Ray, 2021]; see also Baldwin, 2022), and the evident predominance of white and middle-class voices in the movement – while at the same time, Black, Indigenous, and non-white populations are at the knife's edge of the unfolding catastrophe.

In that white, middle-class affect dominates the progressive structure of feeling despite the centrality of anti-racism and of Black and post-colonial thought and action, the intensity of *everything matters now* becomes yet another burden foisted on those for whom the stakes of politics are felt differently. Xine Yao opens *Disaffected: The Cultural Politics of Unfeeling in 19th-Century America*, with a litany: 'White feelings, white tears, white fragility, white women's tears, white men's tears [...] [W]hite feelings produce and maintain structures of domination" (Yao, 2021: 1–2). Yao goes on to argue for the refusal of 'white sentimentality' and proposes *disaffection* as a mode of countering dominant regimes that ceaselessly dramatise white feeling and political agency under the guise of universalism. Such a politics of refusal and withdrawal in the intense present is also central to Hil Malatino's (2022) *Side Affects: On Being Trans and Feeling Bad*, where he writes of the 'selective cultivation of numbness' as a refuge not only from violence and misrecognition but also from the wearing requirements of 'justice-oriented work, as well as the experience of demotivation when this work becomes too much' (Malatino, 2022: 11). In short, the intensity of *everything matters now* is another way that the progressive structure of feeling differentiates, conferring agency and energy to some people, some of the time, while conscripting and draining others. The present is the eye of a storm: raging, and still.

Conclusion: Progressivism without Progress

Caught between a desire to save the world (because "There is no plan(et) B") and a desire for another world (or at least the *possibility* of another world) assembled from the good fragments of the bad past, progressivism participates in the broader cultural phenomenon of apocalyptic politics and the fantasies of world-ending and world-renewing that these perpetuate. Claire Colebrook, in her book on post-apocalyptic cinema, *Who Would You Kill to Save the World?* (2023), writes that: 'In the twenty-first century so many end-of-world dramas have "happy endings" that amount to seeing most of the globe destroyed while a surviving fragment of proper humanity secures a future now redeemed from its less-than-human past' (p. 3). Colebrook connects this dramatic arc to Sylvia Wynter's (2003) critique of how the colonial European system of power and knowledge elevated one particular segment of humanity, one "ethnoclass" (Western, bourgeois Man) to the status of the universal Human. Likewise, Colebrook argues, end-of-world politics elevate a fragment of humanity: the "we" for whom the world threatens to end being also the "we" for whom it has not already ended and the "we" who are heroically tasked with saving it.

While Colebrook and Wynter's critiques are not limited to progressive orientations, we find that this elevation of "a fragment of the present" is critical to progressivism as a structure of feeling that incessantly metabolises the annihilation of worlds, turning these catastrophes into screen images that are projected onto the horizon. In this gesture, the "right action" of progressivism and its promise of a good future are at least momentarily restored, but the tension of progressivism's impasse is only transferred to another site: the interior of its structure of feeling, where the intensity of "everything matters now" overloads those who find themselves nodes in the relay of progressive affect. In order to keep going, progressivism picks over the wreckage of a history of "progress" for shards of hope and projects the worst to the horizon. But there is a cost to this: that in doing so the ancestral catastrophe is disavowed, cast elsewhere (ahead), and the progressive structure of feeling becomes a machine for turning white tears into white redemption, for staving off the annihilation that has already happened as the basis of the "progress" that brought us to our current crisis.

The problem for progressivism is that the good future to which it is necessarily attuned does not seem, after all, to be the destination towards which the winds of change are blowing. To return to Alderman's speculative fiction, *The Power*: 'The voice says: I feel you, but I don't know how to be any clearer about this. You can't get there from here. You'll have to start again' (Alderman, 2016: 330). In a present that feels ever more impassive, progressivism may also take recourse to a multiversal fantasy: the possibility of stepping off the track of this corrupted timeline. Perhaps another world is literally possible, even a Planet B! In the wake of the Brexit referendum and Trump's unexpected (as far as Democrats were concerned) triumph over Hilary Clinton in 2016, jokes about having woken up in a "bad" timeline proliferated online among progressives. On 9 November 2016, *LA Magazine* expressed this fantasy with the headline, 'Great news! In multiverse theory, there are infinite worlds where Donald Trump did not win the election' (Harlander, 2016). No longer convinced by the premise that progress towards justice is inevitable in the long arc of Western history, progressivism finds itself caught in a bad teleology without the engine of its own central concept. Naming a "social justice" left attached to the promise of reparative action in a damaged world while at the same time pinned between ancestral and coming catastrophes and unable to "start again", progressivism is fundamentally troubled *by itself* and its own lacerated affective structure. *What does progress feel like within an impasse?* Agitated by its own contradictions, progressivism somehow finds what it needs in this taut space: its political intensity, its numbness.

4
Liberalism: Defensive, Melancholic, and Boring

Introduction: Liberalism's Affective Crisis

> What a strange paradox that at the very moment "liberal" is enjoying a renaissance. liberalism itself feels on the wane. Many liberals find themselves feeling lonelier than ever. (Paul, 2023, n.p.)

This lament for the loneliness of liberals concludes a 2023 *New York Times* opinion piece. While the word *liberal* is increasingly in use, or so the author claims, these uses are 'confounding', including as disparate and dissonant uses as the revival of 19th-century uses of liberal in the never-Trump conservative right, to the interchangeability of *progressive* and *liberal* that blurs the lines between the two. Liberalism today faces something of an identity crisis. The author's response is to strongly assert liberalism's difference. 'Progressives aren't Liberals', the title proclaims. Although the 'most strenuous threat' of the 'Trumpian right' looms over liberalism, it is progressives who are denounced in the article as dangerously illiberal. They are to blame for why 'liberalism feels itself on the wane'. As progressives and liberals divide in their views on capitalism, white supremacy, and equality, for the author, 'Some aspects of contemporary progressivism look less like actual progress and more like a step in reverse'. Defending liberalism from progressives becomes an urgent task, especially as 'More reactionary still is the repressive nature of progressive ideals around civil liberties'. Facing this lack of love for liberalism, liberal loneliness is part of a present characterised by a resurgent illiberalism, even in those who should have most affinity with liberalism.

Drawing an unambiguous dividing line with progressives is one affective response to liberalism's disorientation in a confounding present. Liberalism in the 2020s remains haunted by multiple losses, none harder to bear than the loss of its own status as beneficiary of the felt sense that "there is no alternative". A set of partially connected events over the last decade – principally the election of Donald J. Trump in 2016 and vote to leave the EU – were felt and interpreted as ruptures with the post 1989 political consensus. History had restarted, with vengeance. Something dangerous had begun amid a maelstrom of post-truth and a resurgence of affectively alluring nativist politics. Part of the eventfulness of these events was their shock to those who were expecting victory and who had sensed in the possibility of either event coming to pass the future spectre of a deeply dangerous illiberalism. Expressions of shock, or just bewilderment, affectively registered the events as unexpected ruptures challenging the continuation of the complex of political and economic liberalism and neoliberalism that had secured a provisional consensus. The present felt a long way from Tony Blair and Bill Clinton era assertions of the inevitability of economic liberalism, from the combination of messianic faith and realist acceptance of globalisation that marked the 1990s. Confounding and devastating in equal measure, the events of 2016 made the end of both economic and political liberalism too affectively present for subjects who, until then, had felt its inevitable continuation. But continuity – in the form of remaining in the European Union or electing Hilary Clinton to follow Barack Obama – had been rejected in favour of the promise of a return to a past that would break with the present. *Make American Great Again* and *Take Back Control* both performing the temporal loop that in Chapter 2 we argued was central to right-wing populism's affective response to the crisis of the future.

In the years since, Brexit and the 2016 election of Trump have been narrated as the beginnings of a potentially terminal crisis in the consensus that knitted political and economic liberalism and neoliberalism. The crisis plays out most intensely in right-wing attacks on political liberalism's creaking rationalities, institutions, and practices, including freedom of speech and individual liberties, due process, democracy, independent judiciary, etc. (see Davies, 2020, for a summary).[1] But it has been intensified by the upsurge of progressivist movements who denounce liberalism for its historical complicity with racial and other structural injustices, critiquing the historical exclusions that accompany and enable liberalism's defining attachment to individual rights and formal equality before the law.[2] Liberal common sense is revealed, through these critiques, as a mechanism for the perpetuation of structural racism and other inequalities. To make sense of liberalism's crisis,

---

[1] Right-wing populist attacks coexist with the return in the present of longstanding conservative critiques of liberalism as responsible for what Deenen (2018: 64) terms an 'anticulture', defined by him as 'the evisceration of culture as a set of generational customs, practices, and rituals that are grounded in local and particular settings' (see Goodhart [2017] for another example of the conservative criticism of liberalism as producing a dangerous absence of belonging and rootedness).

[2] See Losurdo (2014) for a history and critique of the paradoxes of liberalism that make various forms of violence, including indigenous dispossession and endemic anti-Black racism, into the structural accompaniment of liberal (see Seymour 2012 for an iteration of freedom and violence in relation to the 2003 Iraqi war).

multiple attempts have been made by politicians, academics, commentators, and think tanks to characterise what is or might be replacing political liberalism: illiberal democracy; authoritarian neoliberalism (Jessop, 2019), autocratic postdemocracy (Swyngedouw, 2019), and so on (Peck and Theodore, 2019). What matters less than the detail of these diagnostic attempts is their multiplicity, and the sense of the sheer difficulty of naming what is or is not emerging in the present impasse. Alongside these exercises in diagnosis, have been numerous attempts to understand people's dangerous lack of love for liberalism, most prominently around the figure of the urban or rural "left behind", but also in claims of new forms of digital post-truth, dangerous state and non-state actors, or Dominic Cummings, Steve Bannon and other shadowy manipulators of opinion.

What, then, does liberalism become amid its own crisis, as evidence of its failures and rejection pile up and become difficult to absorb or ignore, and as the new politics of intensity we detailed in the previous two chapters takes hold? Crisis is not unique to today's liberalism, in part because political liberalism has since its inception been accompanied by a critique of it as both too little and too much. Liberals have long been criticised for being both too conservative and too progressive. As Gholam Khiabany (2017: 2) summarises, 'For the latter [conservatives], liberalism has gone too far; for the former [progressivists], it has never gone far enough.' For critics, liberalism is *really* a weak copy of a more dangerous political opponent. The term *centrist*, for example, appears synonymous with the incapacity to take and hold a position, of being both and neither, and refusing impassioned calls to commit and take sides.

What makes this conjunctural crisis distinct, though, is that a crisis of political liberalism is articulated with a crisis in neoliberalism's promissory legitimacy and mode of securing consent, if perhaps not in neoliberalism as governing rationality. Rejection of (neo)liberalism as an affect structure is, in part, about the emergence of the new politics of intensity that we have documented in previous chapters, as well as collapsing faith in neoliberal promises as set out in the introduction. But it is also about the slow and fast collapse of the affective complex given the shorthand "there is no alternative" (Fisher, 2009) through which (neo)liberalism secured a degree of provisional, always contested, legitimacy and consent. Forms of passive consent based on acquiescence without attachment appear to be waning. We could say that different forms and styles of affected discontent have replaced the disaffected consent convincingly identified by Jeremy Gilbert (2015; Gilbert and Williams, 2022) as central to post Blair and Clinton neoliberalisms.

In the midst of claims of (neo)liberalism's crisis, we argue that liberalism attempts to return to a near-past with the hope that it could become the future again. Our first proposition is that *liberalism must be defended!* What was once considered common sense now requires defending – a shift that both confirms the emergence of alternatives and sustains the hope that progress remains possible. Next, we home in on liberalism's search for 'good objects' – that is, ideals, institutions, and practices that invite a positive investment of feeling – that might help it to reclaim its previous status as common sense and stir a new love for its promises. In this search, we encounter liberalism's melancholy: *Melancholy, liberalism faces a crisis of attachment.* The good near-past is so close, but none of its well-worn objects of attachment (the institutions of democracy or the promise of equality, for example) can bear the weight of returning liberalism to its hegemonic status, caught as it is in the vice of critiques of liberal elitism from the populist right and of liberalism's failure (especially in relation to racial justice) from the progressive left. Finally, we propose that liberalism's structure of feeling solves its crisis of attachment by offering a particular promise to relatively comfortable subjects: *Liberalism promises nothing ever need change*, including white privilege and the dominance of white affect. If nothing can catalyse a new love for liberalism, liberalism instead offers those who are reasonably content with the status quo the weak hope of being able to get on with life again without having to think or feel too much. Liberalism as a structure of feeling promises the disappearance of a contemporary politics it judges as overfull with intense disagreement and overt contestation. It offers the lure of the return of the end of the political.

Proposition 1: Liberalism Must Be Defended!

Francis Fukuyama proclaims in the opening page of his slim 2022 book, *Liberalism and Its Discontents*, that liberalism now needs to be defended. For the thirty years after *The End of History and the Last Man* (Fukuyama, 1992), this was far from the case. Liberalism had triumphed. The present was diagnosed as post-political. The far-left and far-right appeared to be defeated, as evidenced by the collapse of the Soviet Union, the opening up of Eastern Bloc countries to capitalism, and the rise of centrist-liberal Bill Clinton, and later Tony Blair. But now times have changed: 'The book is intended to be a defence of classical liberalism, or, if the term is too fraught with certain historical connotations, then what Deirdre McCloskey labels 'humane liberalism'. I believe that liberalism is under severe threat around the world today; while it was once taken for granted, its virtues need to be clearly articulated and celebrated once again' (Fukuyama, 2022a: 1).

Fukuyama's defence of liberalism expresses and enacts the troubled position of liberalism today, and the challenges self-identified liberals face. At a time in which liberalism has been declared 'obsolete', and as it is under challenge from both the left and the right, it can no longer be 'taken for granted'. Threats are *everywhere* 'around the world today'. From the right wing, the threat is existential: a growing authoritarianism as the forward march of individual liberty stalls and is reversed in some places. From the left wing, liberalism is made equivalent to neoliberalism and critiqued for the inequalities that have accompanied it and that it engenders. The critique from the position of continued racial injustices haunts defences of liberalism today, even if the starting gun is a defence against the authoritarian populist right.

Fukuyama's short 2020 essay in *American Purpose* from which *Liberalism and Its Discontents* emerged began with the same palpable sense of threat. In Fukuyama's (2020: 1) words, 'Today, there is a broad consensus that democracy is under attack or in retreat in many parts of the world. It is being contested not just by authoritarian states like China and Russia, but by populists who have been elected in many democracies that seemed secure.' In response to this threat, Fukuyama eviscerates both left and right as dangerously illiberal, while at the same time affirming a liberal (rather than progressive) critique of inequality and its need of remedy. For him, both left and right threaten a bad future of fracture and division – a 'deeply divisive future' that shares elements of the catastrophic tone we find in progressivism today.

Fukuyama's is one example of a genre of defence that has emerged as liberalism's taken for granted status collapses, and actors on the left and right declare it obsolete. Defences of liberalism have different objects, moving between the rationalities, practices and institutions that supposedly enable the rights of individuals and the freedom of markets: impartial judicial systems; independent press and media; commitments to free speech; tolerance and dialogue across difference; neutral bureaucracies, and "freedom", to name but the main ones. Defences of political and economic (neo)liberalism may take different forms, but they are always accompanied by grave warnings that liberalism is under threat and often enlivened by troubling examples of liberal principles under attack and being replaced by a resurgent nativist right or an identity politics obsessed left (e.g. Applebaum, 2021).

A key scene of liberal defensiveness that (re)performs this mood, alongside books such as *Liberalism and Its Discontents* that survey the present, has been the public plenary speech given by a political figure closely associated with the near-past of post 1989 liberal triumph. Typically, the statesman diagnoses a world of division and discord and proclaims a return of liberalism as a solution that can restart a temporarily lost progress. Consider the final speech of Obama's presidency, delivered to the United Nations after Trump's election, as an example of the genre of defence which, perhaps inadvertently, helps constitute a sense that "there is an alternative" (Obama, 2016). In the aftermath of the shock of the Trump election, for Obama (articulating a view shared by many) the world is in crisis. After enunciating a range of indicators of 'progress', he identifies a range of forces that lead societies today to be 'filled with uncertainty, and unease, and strife' – a similar diagnosis of the divisive present and precarious future that we hear in Fukuyama and most defences of liberalism:

We see it in the headlines every day. Around the world, refugees flow across borders in flight from brutal conflict. Financial disruptions continue to weigh upon our workers and entire communities. Across vast swaths of the Middle East, basic security, basic order has broken down. We see too many governments muzzling journalists, and quashing dissent, and censoring the flow of information. Terrorist networks use social media to prey upon the minds of our youth, endangering open societies and spurring anger against innocent immigrants and Muslims. Powerful nations contest the constraints placed on them by international law. (Obama, 2016)

The list of events and conditions is a familiar one. Not only is the present in trouble, but a range of tendencies lead to the non-liberal future that haunts Fukuyama's staunch defence of liberalism – a future of division and discord where unreason triumphs.

For Obama, the world faces a moment of choice if it is to avoid a future already taking form in the rancour of the present, one that follows from a 'paradox' of progress coexisting with dissent and discord. The speech continues: 'And so I believe that at this moment we all face a choice. We can choose to press forward with a better model of cooperation and integration. Or we can retreat into a world sharply divided, and ultimately in conflict, along age-old lines of nation and tribe and race and religion' (Obama, 2016). To go forward is, for Obama, to return to the mixture of economic and political liberalism as refracted through neoliberal logics that had until agonisingly recently been the consensus. While, as we saw in the previous chapter, Obama's rhetoric often reproduced the progressive relation with the heroic past, at the end of his presidency it is liberalism alone that can restart the promise of a better future of harmonious progress:

I want to suggest to you today that we must go forward, and not backward. I believe that as imperfect as they are, the principles of open markets and accountable governance, of democracy and human rights and international law that we have forged remain the firmest foundation for human progress in this century. I make this argument not based on theory or ideology, but on facts — facts that all too often, we forget in the immediacy of current events. (Obama, 2016)

Obama's defence of the core tenets of political liberalism, together with the economic liberalism of 'open trade' and free markets, repeats the erasure of liberalism as one ideology among others that was central to its hegemony. 'Facts' are used by Obama to demonstrate that progress *has* happened, improvement attributable to liberalism *is* evident in the present, even if it has been forgotten (and denigrated by progressives). In this move, the superiority of liberalism is re-established and an attempt is made to place it outside the sphere of political contestation.

But the defence is qualified, as all defences of liberalism today inevitably are. Recall how Fukuyama hesitated as he attempted to name what *Liberalism and its Discontent* defends, 'a defence of classical liberalism, *or, if the term is too fraught with certain historical connotations*, then [...] 'humane liberalism' (Fukuyama, 2020: 1, emphasis added). In deference to these unfortunate historical conditions, Obama acknowledges that liberalism has 'neglected' a range of 'real problems', and that as a result 'alternative visions' have 'pressed forward' both in the wealthiest countries and in the poorest. Liberalism must be defended, even if some of the 'facts' suggest something has gone very wrong indeed. And similarly as for Fukuyama, the threats are everywhere, from rich and poor countries and from left and right: 'Religious fundamentalism; the politics of ethnicity, or tribe, or sect; aggressive nationalism; a crude populism – sometimes from the far left, but more often from the far right – which seeks to restore what they believe was a better, simpler age free of outside contamination' (Obama, 2016). Any simple affirmation of liberalism, whatever a speaker takes it to be, is now impossible, as the signs of 'problems' pile up, and its rejection is only too apparent. But in the defence, something important happens. Left and right critiques are rendered equivalent, gathered together in the form of a list – a list that serves as evidence of the problems of an illiberal present.

Liberalism defends itself by, first, asserting and reattaching to past progress, and framing the present as a choice between moving forward or back in linear time. At the same time, it promises that progress will be different in the future. Inequalities, including racial injustices, are a temporary aberration of a liberalism uncharacteristically forgetful of places and people "left behind", rather than a structural consequence of economic (neo)liberalism, the operations of transnational capitalism, and a continuation of the disastrous legacies of slavery and colonialism. By offering the promise of inclusive progress – a progress that leaves no one behind, a progress that empathetically recognises "disruption", a progress once again founded on meritocracy and opportunity – liberalism attempts to secure its own future.

In this liberal future, liberalism, in Obama's words, 'does better'. The promise is that *this time* it will share the benefits and manage the negative effects of global integration and interdependence. Obama insists that, 'Instead [of what happened in the past], we must work together to make sure the benefits of such integration are broadly shared, and that the disruptions – economic, political, and cultural – that are caused by integration are squarely addressed' (Obama, 2016). While progress may be lost to both right-wing populism and progressivism, through the promise of 'doing better' it remains just within reach for liberals. The progress that has happened is attributable to liberalism, and this good trajectory can carry us forward once again, if only the practices, rationalities and institutions of liberalism are defended. And liberalism promises that, this time, things will be different. The critique of liberalism from the perspective of constitutive inequalities, including racial injustice, is dampened by being accepted and translated into the promise that, this time, liberalism will do better. This time it will realise its own promise.

The figure of the white urban and rural "left behind" has been vital to sustaining the hope that in the future liberalism will deliver for all. Being "left behind" serves, first, to explain away the dangerous lack of love for liberalism that seems to mark the present for some subjects. It renders the otherwise bewildering and disturbing detachment from liberalism and attachment to right-wing populism understandable. Edward Luce (2017) in *The Retreat of Western Liberalism,* for example, charges that liberalism became an ideology for the meritocratic elite, forgetting society's "losers". Crystallising in the aftermath of the shock of rejection, the figure of the "left behind" also makes the solution simple: to include all in the warm glow of ever ongoing liberal progress. And the means to deliver that solution is through the liberal rationalities and practices gathered together around tolerance and respect for the other. A whole genre of books and podcasts within and beyond the academy has emerged that involves listening to the voices of the "left behind" with empathy, and accounting for them to audiences attempting to make sense of current conditions and disorientating, disturbing, political events (e.g. Hochschild, 2016; Packer, 2013; 2021). Another genre advocates for a future liberalism that not only listens but changes in response to concerns, most often centred around immigration and the politics of race and ethnicity, such as when Tony Blair, for example, advocates for stricter controls on immigration to 'close off the avenues' of populism (Crerar, 2024a).

In the genre of the liberal defence, as it domesticates the eventfulness of liberalism's various losses, the future as a process of linear improvement is *just about* held onto. It is not irredeemably and permanently lost, but neither is it inevitable any longer. Liberalism might be ending, but not yet. In the present impasse, it is still possible to win or lose. Liberalism might become common sense again, or illiberal forces on the left and right might prevail. If the forward march of globalisation used to be presented by liberals as an inevitability to be adjusted to, now it is a choice to be affirmed if progress is to continue. In this conditionality a hope remains: that the wrong turn everyone (apart from defenders of liberalism) appears to have taken can be corrected, and the present can be returned to the tranquil normality afforded by political and economic liberalism.

Irrespective of what exact mixture of political and economic liberalism is being defended, defences of liberalism are partly constitutive of the end of the atmosphere that "there is no alternative". Only because there are alternatives does liberalism needs defending. As Mark Fisher (2009) showed, the atmosphere or mood that is "there is no alternative" primarily rests on a *negative* claim, rather than positive attachment or investment (although Fisher does emphasise forms of capitalist enjoyment). What he named as 'capitalist realism' is a collective affective quality that emerges through the co-constitutive processes of a collapse in the societal capacity to imagine credible and coherent alternatives to capitalism, pre-emptive delegitimisation of alternatives before they fully emerge, and the creation of value through spectacles of resistance that are pre-incorporated into circuits of capital. That to which there is no alternative does not in itself require justification. Its legitimacy is secured negatively by the maintenance of a lack of belief in the very *possibility* of alternatives.

As soon as liberalism needs to be defended, as soon as critiques are accepted and statements are issued reasserting its superiority even if based on enthusiastic appeals to "facts", then the structure of feeling given the name "there is no alternative" loosens its hold. Liberalism then needs to be clearly defined and articulated, its virtues need to be asserted, and reasons need to be given for why liberalism should triumph, again. Searching for the material for its defence, liberalism rummages around in all kinds of different places, including the pre-history of today's liberalism. For example, Adam Gopnik's (2019) 'stirring defence of liberalism' (to quote from publicity material) finds hope in the lives of people who invented the liberal tradition. And Matt Johnston (2023), in pursuit of a new 'fearless liberalism' in an era of 'counter-enlightenment', looks to the unlikely source of journalist Christopher Hitchen's oeuvre, an idiosyncratic archive that defies easy categorisation but generally drifts from left to right.

No longer confident of its own inevitability, shorn of its special status as both common sense and telos, the necessity and intensity of defence amid a world of threat recalls various post-Second World War scenes of liberalism. In the aftermath of war, the founding text of the American (neo)liberal Mont Pelerin Society, for example, agreed on little other than the presence of threat to the vaguely specified 'central values of civilization':

> The central values of civilization are in danger. Over large stretches of the Earth's surface the essential conditions of human dignity and freedom have already disappeared. In others they are under constant menace from the development of current tendencies of policy. The position of the individual and the voluntary group are progressively undermined by extensions of arbitrary power. Even that most precious possession of Western Man, freedom of thought and expression, is threatened by the spread of creeds which, claiming the privilege of tolerance when in the position of a minority, seek only to establish a position of power in which they can suppress and obliterate all views but their own. (Mont Pelerin Society, 1947)

Amplifying the state-phobia that neoliberalism inherits from classical liberalism (Foucault, 2008), a series of objects of attachment orientated around 'western man' are felt as being under threat in a moment of danger. Fascism and communism are made into the same problem – the overmighty state in distinction from the individual and groups of individuals. From this cauldron of imminent threat and other atmospheres, something that became neoliberalism began to take form.

Other post-World War II defences of political and economic liberalism share this sense of threat with the nascent neoliberalism of the Mont Pelerin Society, as well as the rendering equivalent the right and left. Arthur Schlesinger's (1948) post-war conception of the 'vital center', for example, rested on a sense of threat from all sides. The 'vital center' is distinguished from both left and right, while being composed of elements from both. Left and right are outdated ideas, Schlesinger claims, as he finds an anti-individual extremism in both 'left and right fascism'. Defined first negatively, the 'center' names the point of connection between what Schlesinger calls 'the non-communist Left' and 'non-fascist Right'. Schlesinger identifies this 'vital center' as key to the future of America, but also always-already under threat from the 'extremes':

> For hope of the future surely lies in the revival of the Center – in the triumph of those who believe deeply in civil liberties, in constitutional processes and in the democratic determination of political and economic policies. And, in direct consequence, the main target of both totalitarian extremes must be the Center – the group which hold society together. Neither fascism nor communism can win so long as there remains a democratic middle way, which unites hopes of freedom and of economic abundance; so the destruction of the middle way becomes the first priority for both. (Schlesinger, 1948).

Inseparable from the hopes of freedom and abundance, 'the center' is from its invention a political position already-always precarious, facing threats from all sides. It can never be secure, because of its position between "extreme" left and right, rejecting both, but being composed of various mixtures of each.

We hear in Obama and Fukuyama's defence of liberalism the same hope in the 'center' that Schlesinger articulated in the ruins of a cataclysmic world war. For him, as for Obama and Fukuyama today, it is the 'center' that holds out against both left and right, both of which constitute 'extremes'. Schlesinger concludes his piece advocating for the 'vital center' by citing W.B. Yeats' line from *The Second Coming* that the 'worst are full of passionate intensity'. His hope is that the 'vital center' can discover the same intensity in the post-war period: 'The problem of United States policy is to make sure that the Center does hold; and this can be done only by supporting it against all blandishments and all threats, from whatever direction they may come. The best must recover a sense of principle; and, on the basis of principle, they may develop a passionate intensity. We cannot afford to loose the blood-dimmed tide ever again' (Schlesinger, 1948).

In the present, liberals repeat Schlesinger hope for liberal passion. Defences of elements of liberalism are, at the same time, paradoxical calls for people to reattach to something they perhaps never attached to, and to do so with feeling. The longing for people to find a regularly lost 'passionate intensity' for liberalism plays out across different liberal defences. Reminiscent of calls for a 'muscular liberalism' in the aftermath of 9/11, Blair charges that liberalism has become 'flabby and unwilling to take people on', as the West is consumed by guilt. The centre needs to change tone, to move away from guilt and apology and embrace defence and celebration. When Blair declares that 'One of the problems with the West is that it constantly can be made to feel guilty about itself – and I'm not saying there aren't things we should feel guilty about. But you know, we shouldn't let people intimidate us into thinking there are certain values we shouldn't be standing up for' (Blair quoted by Coughlan, 2016), what comes across is a somewhat desperate hope that people will 'stand up' for values that, only recently, needed no defence – values he still associates with 'the West' per se.

In a 2022 piece for the *Financial Times*, Fukuyama finds the same type of hope in the dividing lines offered by Russian aggression in Ukraine. Positively heralded by a range of commentators and politicians as a multinational defence of the liberal world order,[3] the Ukrainian war supposedly provides the kind of clarifying event liberals have long needed to reassert faith in a project under threat. The Ukrainian war promises to deliver the clarifying passionate intensity that some pro-war liberals had previously found in the good and evil binaries and democratising mission of the "war on terror" (Seymour, 2012). One problem for those defending liberalism, Fukuyama claims, is that 'the virtues of living in a liberal world have been taken for granted by many' (Fukuyama, 2022b). Paradoxically, the rejection of liberalism is because life is *too liberal*. Liberalism's very success breeds the conditions for its rejection, even if liberalism still remains the 'last best hope' of overcoming the divisions that scar the present (Packer, 2021). Echoing the longstanding connection between masculinity and the revelatory truth of war, Fukuyama finds in responses to

---

[3] The support for Ukraine was performed through a material and digital culture of flags on public buildings and social media platforms. Despite waning public interest as the war continued, it re-intensified during the 2024 UK General Election campaign as Nigel Farage's questioning of support for the war became an occasion for both the Labour and Conservative Parties to express unlimited, unconditional, support.

Ukrainian resistance an inspiration that might become something grander, a new mood: a 'revival of the spirit of 1989'. He concludes:

> The travails of liberalism will not end even if Putin loses. China will be waiting in the wings, as well as Iran, Venezuela, Cuba and the populists in western countries. But the world will have learnt what the value of a liberal world order is, and that it will not survive unless people struggle for it and show each other mutual support. The Ukrainians, more than any other people, have shown what true bravery is, and that the spirit of 1989 remains alive in their corner of the world. For the rest of us, it has been slumbering and is being reawakened. (Fukuyama, 2022b)

Proposition 2: Melancholy, Liberalism Faces a Crisis of Attachment

Hoping that the cataclysmic destruction of war between nation-states might help revive something called the "spirit of 1989" exemplifies the bind liberals face as they defend and celebrate what had become common sense. The liberal object of attachment is located in the past before liberalism was in crisis, but the past is so near that it feels like a no-hard-feelings return is still possible. And yet this return to the near past that promises to restart progress is regularly frustrated by threats from both left and right in the present. The desperate hope is that war will clarify what is at stake and catalyse a love for liberalism that would be more than the acquiescence or grudging acceptance that marked consent for liberalism (for lack of an alternative) before this conjunctural crisis.

Liberalism faces, then, a crisis of attachment that it struggles to solve as it passionately, intensely, attempts to return itself to the status of common sense. The bind liberals find themselves in begins from an intensification of attachment to a cluster of liberal objects that have either been replaced or rejected in the present or were just never really that intensely attached to as forms of passive consent took hold. In liberalism's story of itself as a triumphant force for good, a set of familiar liberal objects are held out as promises: the rule of law, tolerance of difference, individualism, the market economy. Their value is repeatedly reasserted in performances of heightened attachment that pays little mind to the progressive critique of liberalism's structural whiteness. The British political commentator Ian Dunt's 2020 *How to Be a Liberal*, for example, tells a passionate story of how liberalism triumphed over the twin evils of modernity – the fascism of Nazi Germany and communism of the Soviet Union – such that liberalism appears as that which has set the world right in the past and can do so again.

But this parade of liberal goodness cannot drown out the clamour of its collapse. Too much evidence abounds that not only have specific liberalisms deteriorated institutionally but also liberalism's traditional structure of feeling – its confidence in its own singular rightness – has become shaky. Even defences of the values and principles of liberalism now must be qualified with regrets for people and places "left behind" and promises that if we can all just get behind liberalism again, *this time* things really will be meritocratic, there really will be opportunities for all. Within this defensive crouch, liberals maintain a frustrated attachment to a near-past that is felt and remembered as *good*. Blair era New Labour was associated with the flourishing of 'cool Britannia', and a revival of a national optimism that felt quite different to the vengeful nationalisms and nativist politics that scar the present. Obama promised a multi-racial democracy without the intensity of having to reckon with ongoing racial injustice, and a renewed hope that justice and the dynamics of free market capitalism were compatible. Social democratic measures served as signs of care that contrast sharply with the diminishment of material resources and expectations that mark austerity's slow and fast violences. Just like the "spirit of 1989", this remembered good past is *close,* rather than impossible in the case of progressives or distant but not yet lost in the case of right-wing populists.

In the aftermath of the advent of neoliberalism and after the supposed "end of history", Wendy Brown (2000) identified left melancholia as a dominant 'structure of desire' animating parts of the organised left in Western Europe and North America. The malaise of parts of the left at this time was diagnosed by Brown around an impossible attachment to a better tomorrow that would be rooted in the return of a range of 'crushed ideals, signified by the terms "left", "socialism", "Marx", or "movement"' (Brown, 2000: 23). Amid multiple accountable, unaccountable, unavowed and unavowable losses of and for the left, yearning for a crushed ideal replaced attachment to a better future, and a capacity to orientate to and seize political opportunities in the present. Left melancholia involves a stuckness:

Left melancholia represents not only a refusal to come to terms with the particular character of the present, that is, a failure to understand history in terms other than "empty time" or "progress". It signifies as well a certain narcissism with regard to one's past political attachments and identity that exceeds any contemporary investment in political mobilization, alliance, or transformation. (Brown, 2000: 22)

We could say left melancholia was a constitutive part of the atmosphere that was "there is no alternative", since it also involved the absence of the future as scene of novelty and rupture that would usher in something new. However, in the previous chapter we proposed that progressivism can no longer be characterised in terms of left melancholia; indeed, its intense re-emergence might be precisely because attachment to the ideals of the economistic, Marxist left has faded (too masculinist, too white, too unable to galvanise a fragmented "left behind" working class). The urgent focus on the present has solved the problem of attachment for progressives, for whom the past is a set of good fragments of justice deferred and the future is now an onrushing catastrophe that requires emergency action to avoid.

Instead, melancholia – the feeling arising from a continued attachment to an almost loss object – has become central to today's liberal structure of feeling. For even as they find themselves forced to face up to history starting again, liberals remain attached to that which is being rejected and replaced. We could say that, at the moment when progressivists find new intensity at the eye of the storm of the unfolding catastrophe, liberalism takes up the sense of loss that was once central to progressives. What exactly liberals are attached to is an open question, one complicated by the vagueness of the term *liberal*, the multiplicity of economic and political liberalisms and the complex relations of these with neoliberalisms, which are themselves always-already plural.[4] The idolised near-past object is multiple but also vague, existing sometimes in definite

---

[4] Indeed, all current defences of liberalism involve careful qualification of what liberalism is not, in particular how it relates to neoliberalism and market freedoms (e.g. see Gopnik's [2019] insistence that he is absolutely not a neoliberalism, something that he doesn't really think is something anyway, more a bogeyman' or 'swearword' for childish radicals).

institutional arrangements and practices, and at other times surfacing atmospherically as something closer to an almost lost sense of how a past present used to feel: a series of norms of action and interaction governing the conduct of formal politics; stability in institutions; a period of calm and seeming stability; political leaders who inspire and in whom one can invest national pride; a country that was improving; the rule of law; optimism for a better tomorrow; everything working.

The good liberal near-past that has come to exemplify and express this inchoate mix of promises is just about locatable in a time after the defeat of socialism *and* after the worst excesses of Reaganism and Thatcherism were alleviated. In this lull, (neo)liberal capitalism assumed the status of felt inevitability. It is the phase of neoliberalism associated with the roll out of various protective measures that allowed the worst excess of capitalism to remain hidden for some subjects, in contrast to the evident brutality of today's newly "illiberal" or "authoritarian" neoliberalism (Brown, 2019). It is a time marked by a social liberalism and cosmopolitanism. It becomes unsettled by liberal wars as part of the "war on terror" and runs aground with the 2008 financial crisis. It is a time so close that many of the political figures are still active, albeit at the margins of political discourse, occasionally surfacing to defend liberalism. Culturally, it is felt in the extension of the "long 90s" through an economy of stadium tours, re-releases, tribute acts, nostalgia nights, and cultural figures.[5]

---

[5] The "long 90s" is a phrase used by the British Left to diagnose the cultural politics of the neoliberal consensus, a mixture of cultural sterility and intense technological change See Stream #ACFM Trip 16: The Long '90s by Novara Media https://novaramedia.com/2021/05/23/acfm-trip-16-the-long-90s/

Melancholia ossifies and reifies, as Brown (2000: 23, via Benjamin, 1931/1994) stresses. Liberal melancholia invests in this tantalisingly close past, even as liberalism's contingent errors are acknowledged and calls to listen to the "left behind" proliferate. By identifying the presence of liberal melancholia, we can better understand the relation liberals have with progressivism and right-wing populism. In a process of affective transfer, liberal self-reproach for its failure is transferred into anger and resentment at others who become responsible for the non-return of the not quite lost near-past. Despite their intimacy, we get a sense here of why particular figures of the progressive left are often subject to the most bellicose critiques by liberals, even as the critique from the left that the free-market economy has failed some subjects is accepted. For it is the progressive left who are most responsible for denying the return to the almost but not quite lost past, and whose lack of love for liberalism is most difficult to comprehend given that liberalism so clearly provides the path to the good, right, and true. In this, the whiteness of liberalism is reproduced. Because it brought about the good near-past and remains the hope for the future, liberalism cannot be held responsible for past and ongoing structural harms and damages. Continued racial injustices and inequalities, most notably, can never be accepted as a structural part of liberalism, if liberalism is to remain the path to the future. Cast as the ones who bear the costs of liberalism's failures – failures that are understood to be a contingent aberration rather than structural feature – or as deprived souls more susceptible to manipulation, the white "left behind" supporters of populists are more understandable to liberals than the progressive left. The flipside of the figure of the "left behind" to be listened to are the "extreme" left who must be aggressively delegitimised if liberalism is to become common sense again. Note, for example, liberal disdain for the pro-Palestinian university encampments and the intensity of attack that both Jeremy Corbyn and Bernie Saunders were subject to from liberal commentators.

It is not just figures of the left who attract liberal anger and resentment. A seemingly endless cast of characters are invoked to explain the dangerous lack of love for liberalism: Dominic Cummings, Steve Bannon, Russia, Facebook, postmodernism, etc. Channelling resentment and anger around specific figures allows the dangerous lack of love for liberalism to be explained in a way that conserves liberal objects from scrutiny and loss. Better, for example, to repeat the longstanding trope of the Machiavellian, backstage manipulator and make a figure like Dominic Cummings into an object of fascination, than to ask how a liberal object of attachment like the EU could be rejected. And, of course, the fascination with Machiavellian figures perhaps brings its own enjoyment, making some of the pleasures of conspiracism available to liberals: the pleasure of reestablishing simple lines of causation and morality and reinforcing a clear distinction between the enlightened and the manipulated masses.

Alongside this displacement of scrutiny are attempts to reactivate ossified promissory objects that once were part of the background of "there is no alternative". A prime example of this reactivation of almost-lost objects manifests in the present-day intense concern with the distorting effects of "fake news" and disinformation. Underneath the diagnosis of the present in terms of "post-truth" is the performance of a continued attachment to a range of different liberal objects. The first is a clear divide not only between true and false but also between "truth" and the glut of opinion. The second, and as important, is the promise of the public sphere as a realm of reasoned disagreement between equals, all of whom commit to truthfulness. In this formulation, "truth" is not only the opposite of both falsity and opinion, but also of *feeling*. As Megan Garber writes in *The Atlantic*'s 'If Trump Wins' collection, 'Every story Trump invents—every wild claim, freed from the dull weight of accuracy—doubles as permission: You, too, can feel your way to your facts' (Garber, 2023).

With liberalism facing off against both falsity and unreason, there has evolved a minor public culture of liberal journalists "defending" truth, for example *Post-Truth: The New War on Truth* by Mathew D'Ancona (2017) or *Post-Truth: Why We Have Reached Peak Bullshit* by Evan Davis (2017).[6] In these and other cases, "post-truth" is the diagnostic tool used to make sense of why *other people* have succumbed to the force of unreason. In the midst of upheaval, post-truth offers the comfort that the problem is an old one that liberalism has long been in combat with – the unreason of others. Even if the conditions for the production of unreason are new, drawing in everything from Russia to digital mediation of life and given new names such as "fake news", the problem is one that liberals know well and have vanquished before: the masses have been manipulated by demagogues. How else to explain why people voted for

---

[6] D'Ancona and Davies are examples of an intensified interest in post-Truth, primarily to try and get to grips with the events of Brexit and Trump's first election (for other examples of popular books in the same period by broadly liberal commentators and journalists see Ball (2017); Levitin (2017)). The genre included anxious articles on how to identify "fake news" (such as *The Guardian's* 2016 piece on 'What is fake news? How to spot it and what you can do to stop it' [Hunt, 2016]) as well as a backlash claiming that the set of terms, specifically "fake news", weren't helping solve the problem they purported to name (such as *Slate*'s appeal to 'Stop calling everything fake news' [Oremus, 2016]). In 2016, post-truth was declared Oxford Dictionaries' 'word of the year' (Oxford Languages, 2016).

Trump or for Brexit, and rejected the progress liberalism had given them? The promise is not, then, simply a return to "truth", but a return to the clarity of being able to divide reason from unreason. And it is a return to the dividing line between the demagogue who manipulates and the liberal who is rational and right. More than anything, the claim of "post-truth" allows attachment to a very simple liberal object: that liberalism is the good, right, and true. It allows an explanation for why actors seem to have rejected liberalism despite all the evidence of its responsibility for "progress" in the near-past.

But what appears simple is also treacherous, because "truth" and "reason" (like other liberal objects of attachment) have become slippery in the digitally mediated present. Even books that denounce them acknowledge that some of the contemporary forms and practices gathered under the name "post-truth" or "fake news" *feel* good and are effective. Recognising that subjects want and need to be affected, Matthew D'Ancona (2017), for example, argues for countering the affective vividness of unreason by wrapping *facts* with experience, memory and hope. The other problem with defending truth from post-truth is that what lies on one side or the other is never easily settled and the lines between conspiracy theory and critique blur. This is evident in Brexit supporters' denunciation of the Remain campaign as 'Project Fear', implying that this liberal campaign was not spreading "facts" but attempting to manipulate public emotion. And nobody is more incensed by FAKE NEWS than Trump himself, as his capitalised tweets broadcast.

Finally, the claim that the era of post-truth began in 2006 belies the breakdown of the lines between fact and value, between reason and construction, that extends back at least into the advent of the "war on terror", and so colours the almost lost past of liberal melancholia (Massumi, 2015). This bleed leads to a somewhat desperate attempt by commentators to draw ever finer lines between different versions of unreason, admitting some might have been part of politics for longer than the present turbulence. Davis (2017), for example, makes distinctions between post-truth, nonsense, post-fact, and gibberish. It also means that the cast of characters responsible for this unfortunate descent into anti-liberal unreason extends somewhat erratically backwards and forwards in time as commentators try to make their claims make sense. Matthew D'Ancona (2017) blames 'postmodernism' (a cultural movement that had its heyday in the 1970s and 1980s), for example. Occasionally, doubts surface about why truth and post-truth have become of such concern in the present moment, just as they do in the caveats and regrets that surface in defences of liberalism. Evan Davis (2017: xviii), for example, wonders whether concern with post-truth is just 'an expression of frustration and anguish from a liberal class discombobulated by the political disruptions of 2016'. If "truth" itself cannot bear the weight of liberal attachment, it is perhaps better understood as a diagnostic tool for understanding why subjects do not act and think as liberals do. Rather than being its own good, it allows reattachment to the most circular of promissory objects – liberalism itself – which will return if only the forces of unreason are vanquished.

Other more positive promissory objects have emerged from within the frenzy of the turbulent present, but they also reflect an attempt to reanimate ossified, not-quite-lost objects. For example, one that was central to the post-Brexit culture in the UK was the "EU". After the decision to exit the EU, and in the long impasse between decision and exit, a political culture emerged in the UK advocating first to stay in and now to rejoin the EU. Central to this political culture was an intensified attachment to the "EU" that had at best been residual over the past forty years, as popular variants of Euroscepticism dominated UK political life.

In the impasse between referendum and exit, the "EU" was newly rehabilitated as an object of attachment. A set of previously unknown public figures united by and known only for the strength of their attachment to the EU emerged to temporary micro-stardom: Steve Bray, Femi Oluwole, Gina Miller. First as part of the 'people's vote' campaign, and now as part of the smaller re-join movement, large scale marches were held in central London. And a whole commercial culture of hats, clothing, objects, and badges emerged, together with a liberal cultural sphere of podcasts and books. The "EU" was thus made to stand in for and translate liberalism's inchoate mix of promises and desired objects: the hope of an alternative to a vengeful nationalism then taking shape globally; a passionate faith in the will of the people, that resonates with the same claim within the right-wing populism that Brexit was symptom and enactment of; an undemanding, easy multiculturalism founded in tolerance and dialogue that does not have to confront structural inequalities; something other to then political demagogues, and so on.

But there was something else going on as well. The songs of 'EU Supergirl' exemplify this something else. EU Supergirl is the stage name of Madeleina Kay, who became a minor celebrity within the EU Remain/re-join culture, playing at marches, touring Europe, and debating Brexiters during live television appearances. Before a video featuring scenes from a Remainer protest, with protesters draped in EU flags, her song 'Don't hold back' preaches defiance, finishes with the line 'Don't hold back it's not over yet'.[7] The message is to keep going because, ultimately, you will be proved right. History is still on your side. It has just branched out in an unfortunate way, but the course can

---

[7] Don't Hold Back – Madeleina Kay (youtube.com).

be corrected. One of the hashtags of the current fading UK rejoin moment – #wetoldyouso – performs this same confidence that, sooner or later, people will realise the error of their ways. Across this culture, EU membership becomes the almost-lost object that cannot be given up. If you just keep going for long enough, in the future things will go back to the way they were before the unfortunate and temporary deviation of exit.

Reattaching to truth and the EU promise a return to the near-past when history had ended and liberalism was comfortably common sense. Both identify something lost – truth, EU membership – and an error, which if only it could be corrected would enable history to end again. The promise underneath this attempt to make existing liberal objects – practices such as dialogue, institutions such as the EU – into promissory objects is a simple one: the good near-past can be returned to if only we can convince others to attach passionately to what had previously been in the background of their lives.

What emerges alongside these attempts to end history by fostering attachment to past objects is a culture of public mockery and denigration from both right and left that alights upon the stuckness of liberalism and the absurdity of its objects of attachment. From the right, the charge of "remoaner" dismissed as pathetic both the attachment to the EU and warnings of the post EU future. Together with the refrain of 'Project Fear', the charge was that liberalism lacked the proper affective relation with the post-EU future. Instead of the negative hope and national optimism that gathered around the event of Brexit (see Anderson et al., 2020), liberalism, as refracted through its re-attachment to the "EU", was judged as only able to relate to the future as threat. Liberals were charged with a dangerous lack of faith in Britain and its future.

From the progressive left, it was the attachment to the culture of the near-past that was the object of mockery and critique. The "centrist Dad" meme, for example, emerged in the mid-late 2010s from the internal politics of the Labour Party as amplified by a nascent left-wing political meme culture. It mocked an over attachment to a mid-1990s/early 2000s political-cultural period, while critiquing the performance of a form of condescending political masculinity that restored whiteness to centre stage. Resonating with longstanding critiques from the left of cultural sterility, the meme named and mocked a culture that refused to face change, including its own end. "Centrist" and "Dad" were both deployed as mild insults. Occasionally, attempts were made to rehabilitate the phrase. Being a centrist was promoted as an antidote to the problem of intensified polarisation (e.g. Alun Cochrane 'Centrist Dad', BBC Sounds). But in the main, the meme became part of a wider online left-wing culture that skewered liberalism, including from the American "dirtbag" left such as Chapo Trap House. Defensive and replying with paranoid explanations for its own rejection and catastrophic warnings of future, liberalism was mocked as a culture of stuckness – stuck in its politics, stuck in its culture, stuck in its melancholy attachment to a near-past.

Proposition Three: Liberalism Promises That Nothing Ever Need Change

Mockery of the stuckness of liberalism from both left and right is partly one affective form that their shared rejection of liberalism takes today. But it also testifies to the serious problem of attachment that liberalism faces. As the sense that "there is no alternative" engulfed political life post 1989, liberal objects – "truth", "the rule of law", "reasoned discussion", "dialogue" – slowly faded as objects of attachment. Only with difficulty can they now be reanimated as promises that people intensely attach to, especially when it is the very near-past which has been rejected, and alternatives proliferate. How else, then, does liberalism attempt to solve its crisis of attachment, if the "spirit of 1989", "truth", and other past objects are unlikely to generate the passionate intensity liberalism needs today? And how does it do so amid intense challenges from the populist right, but also from the progressive left, and especially the intense critique of liberalism's failure to right the wrongs of white supremacy? With loss and threat on every side, liberalism offers the opposite of attachment: the promise of detachment and the comforting sense that nothing ever need change after all. The demands of the present, including the demand for redress and reckoning with liberalism's injustices need not really be confronted. The present can be quiet again, just like the near past – at least for those not facing inequality, for those not living ongoing structural harms.

During Joe Biden's 2020 presidential campaign, Obama jokingly offered American voters the promise of detaching from the too raucous realm of politics. Worn down by the culture that surrounded Trump, exhausted by the sheer excess of it all, the offer was of a detachment that hadn't been possible during Trump's first presidency:

'With Joe and Kamala you're not going to have to think about the crazy things they say every day,' said Obama. 'It just won't be so exhausting. You might be able to have a Thanksgiving dinner without having an argument.' He added: 'You'll be able to go about your lives knowing that the president is not going to retweet conspiracy theories about secret cabals running the world or that Navy SEALs didn't actually kill bin Laden. Think about that. The president of the United States retweeted that.' (Obama quoted in Shepherd, 2020)

Obama's promise happened alongside other normative promises that gathered around Biden, including heteronormative positioning of him as father and grandfather, together with a return to a politics of growth, but this time with opportunity for all. The promise of not having to think anymore was telling for how it marked the Trump period out as an aberration, a time of excess for the sheer presence of politics in people's everyday life. Unlike in the near-past, in the time of Trump, you *couldn't not think about politics*. Even worse, it was increasingly difficult to avoid getting caught up in political passions, becoming agitated, becoming part of discord and division. Trump and politics were everywhere, including in the scenes of ordinary celebration Obama evoked. In the UK, the Conservative's 2019 general election slogan – Get Brexit Done – played on a similar desire for resolution and the hope that a period of public political tumult might end.

This is a hope that seems to continually blossom anew. The promise of not feeling was not only embodied by Biden but lurked in the background to recent political changes in the UK, as Rishi Sunak replaced Boris Johnson and Keir Starmer Jeremy Corbyn. Both were initially lauded for the lack of intensity and tumult that they supposedly brought to the realm of the political. Before his shift to an incoherent mix of right-wing populism and economic liberalism in the period before the 2024 UK General Election, Sunak was heralded for his lack of flare. British print and broadcast media highlighted his supposed "pragmatism" and "invisibility". Being invisible promised to pay out a 'dullness dividend', a term supposedly invented in the City of London. The claim was that 'scarcely being seen' generated political value after the turbulence of Liz Truss. Unlike his immediate predecessors, Sunak's absence from the public was valued as implicitly what people desired from a politician. In an editorial, *The Times* urged readers to not 'Underestimate the dullness dividend' associated with Sunak and his chancellor Jeremy Hunt (Editorial *The Times*, 12 March 2023). The *Financial Times* even suggested that the dullness dividend had the real financial impact of lowering long-term borrowing rates, in comparison to the 'moron premium' associated with Liz Truss (Giles and Parker, 2022).

Boredom was also integral to Keir Starmer's promise as Labour leader. After the Labour Party conference of 2023, briefings pivoted to make a virtue of Starmer's boringness. At least if nothing was happening, nothing could get worse than it already was. Being a 'man without qualities', as one sceptical commentator from the left put it, might turn out to be a good thing in an over intense present (Scothorne, 2022). Starmer's boringness, the absence of anything too excessive, was something to be promoted. In an interview on BBC Radio 4's *Today* programme, after stressing that the most exciting moment of his life was the birth of his children, Starmer invoked the precariousness of the present:

When we're facing a period of great uncertainty and we've got conflict in Ukraine, we've got a cost-of-living crisis, we've got a government that's lost control the economy, do we need a serious person steering the country calmly and confidently to a better future? I think the answer to that is yes. 'If I came on and said I'd done a bungee jump, you wouldn't say 'Great, now we've got the prime minister we need'. (Starmer, quoted by Woodcock, 2022).

The same claim returned in commentaries on Biden's re-election effort. A *Rolling Stone* article entitled 'boredom is good' made the case for Biden's boringness, praising Biden for his stability and for 'turning down the heat' (Michaelson, 2023). For Michael Schaffer, writing in *Politico* in 2022, Biden kept his promise to be boring: 'It was a key theme of Joe Biden's 2020 campaign, unstated but powerful, and a vivid contrast with the public-train-wreck incumbent: If elected, he was going to be boring' (Schaffer, 2022). In comparison with the sheer unavoidable intensity of Trump, Biden seemed to perform a 'cardboard presidency'.

In little remarked upon comments laced with melancholy, even Fukuyama, in the essay of the same title that preceded *The End of History* book, speculated that the threat of eternal boredom might yet restore history's momentum: 'Perhaps this very prospect of centuries of boredom at the end of history will serve to get history started once again' (Fukuyama, 1989: 18). The low-level irritation or unease of boredom is what remains after the distinctive "end" that Fukuyama argued constitutes liberalism. History ended because, for Fukuyama, liberalism satisfied desires for both equal recognition and material prosperity. Uniquely, liberal democracies were without the 'contradictions' that drove historical progress (and here Fukuyama's Hegelian influence comes out). What was left, though, was a kind of surplus desire for something more. As he put it: '... the post-historical world is one in which the desire for comfortable self-preservation has been elevated over the desire to risk one's life in a battle for prestige, and in which universal and rational recognition has replaced the struggle for domination' (Fukuyama, 1992: 283). Something like boredom was how this unsatisfied desire registered affectively, although it alone would not be enough to get history restarted again, given that all the 'contradictions' of politics and economics had, Fukuyama claimed somewhat implausibly, been resolved.

In this present, Fukuyama's question is reversed. Perhaps an outbreak of political boredom is precisely what is needed to end history again, liberals wonder and hope. A period of dullness led by politicians without qualities is promoted as the antidote to the too much bad intensity that characterises left and right in the contemporary political scene. Boredom would allow detachment from the toxicity of the present, but also the demands for change that give the present its intensity.

Boredom blurs here with a longstanding valuation of liberal dispassion, and forms of cultivated detachment from positions that are felt by others as too much (Anderson, 2000). Writing against the spectre of discord and division, and coexisting a touch uncomfortably with his call to find again the 'spirit of 1989', Fukuyama celebrates the lack of intensity he associates with tolerance:

The most fundamental principle enshrined in liberalism is one of tolerance: you do not have to agree with your fellow citizens about the most important things, but only that each individual should get to decide what they are without interference from you or from the state. Liberalism lowers the temperature of politics by taking questions of final ends off the table: you can believe what you want, but you must do so in private life and not seek to impose your views on your fellow citizens. (Fukuyama, 2022c)

"Lowering the temperature" of politics is, though, a bit of a problem if, at the same time, you are looking to rekindle a currently lost love for liberalism as a way of returning something to the status of background common sense. As Fukuyama acknowledges, 'Moreover, liberalism can be uninspiring to many people. A doctrine that deliberately lowers the sights of politics and enjoins tolerance of diverse views often fails to satisfy those who want strong community based on shared religious views, common ethnicity or thick cultural traditions' (Fukuyama, 2022c: n.p.). Perhaps the promise of dispassion contains the seeds of its own failure, both because it may pale next to a promise of intensity and because it is not that easy to achieve. Boredom is an ambivalent phenomenon, not equivalent to dispassion. Boredom is intimate with low-level affects of minor aversion – irritation and frustration, for example – that involve a movement from and often rejection of that which bores. So, being boring is rarely welcomed by those accused of it, particularly given the shift to affective forms of political leadership where politicians now routinely mobilise a range of affective styles in addition to charisma.[8] Both Sunak and Starmer were regularly mocked for their boringness, with their dullness betraying an absence of ideas, and an incapacity to grasp the profound challenges of the present.

More than this, liberal commentators appeared to be nervous about whether the public actually wanted more or less intensity. Perhaps, secretly, terrifyingly, people wanted to be outraged, and actually *enjoyed* the post-truth spectacles of excess and exuberance from left and right. A *Vanity Fair* article praises and worries about Biden's boringness in the context of a news media attached to excitement: 'The problem for Team Biden is that its superpower, its ability to slide under the radar while getting a lot done for the American people, may also be its Achilles heel, holding back the administration from getting the credit it deserves' (Jong-Fast, 2023). Biden might have kept his promise to be boring, but for Schaffer (2022) in *Politico*, that has a 'drawback': 'A boring presidency is, um, boring.'[9] Performing this confusion about what the public want, the politicians described as boring and those speaking on their

---

[8] See Pedwell (2014) for an analysis of the performance of empathy in liberal and neoliberal political leadership, for example.

[9] During the 2024 presidential election, Biden's boringness was overshadowed by the uncertainty that followed from concern about his age, his physical and cognitive precarity. The offer of the withdrawal from the political into stability and a minimal optimism was undermined by the insecurity that followed from the question of how, if at all, he'd be able to perform the role of president.

behalf both rejected the charge of being boring, celebrating it as a deft political strategy rather than a failure to inspire. At one stage, Keir Starmer let it be known that the shadow cabinet was to stop briefing the press that he was 'boring' (Stewart, 2022). What was *really* boring, he claimed, was opposition.

The question of whether a politician's blandness is a good or bad thing, whether it is to be welcomed or rejected, is symptomatic of liberalism's affective crisis. As well as simply providing an affective contrast with other politicians, political boredom offers the promise of being able to return to being the post-political subject of disaffected consent. You don't need to identify or invest in a leader or political strategy, you can disagree or be frustrated, but, whatever the relation, it will all feel so much less intense than politics has. You can detach from it all, if you wish. Political boredom offers a new promise – withdrawal from the turbulent, bewildering present. It offers the promise of not having to think or feel about all that is happening and might happen. It offers the promise of not having to worry about those subjects and groups for whom the near-past wasn't good. The ability to attach to the promise that there will be *no need to feel anything anymore* differentiates those who can access this 'boredom' and those who find themselves unable to be lulled by this promise – whether due to the continued precarity of their lives, their active fear of catastrophic futures, or their alienation from the unspoken normativity of liberal calm and what must go uncontested to maintain it.

Liberalism's performance of boringness offers a solution to the "real" problem: too many raucous, unruly, demands from which there is no escape. Others are too invested, there are too many heightened and heated disagreements, too much intensity. Both progressivism and populism are too much, introducing the too much of fake news, conspiracy, cancellation, authoritarianism, mass rallies, demands for racial justice, and irrationality into formal politics. Liberalism offers calm. It brings an affective "dullness dividend" while at the same time offering the heady pleasure of judging other's passions. And it offers detachment from a politics which has become too much. Liberalism offers not needing to think any more about politics, exiting the space of disagreement and contestation, and just being able to get on with life. Yes, this is in part a response to the too much of a resurgence form of authoritarian right-wing populism that legitimatises resentment fuelled anger, as we argued in Chapter 2. But it is also a response to demands from the progressive left, including for a reckoning with forms of racial injustice and the legacies of dispossession. It enables life to carry on as before. Before the conjunctural crisis and the cracking of common sense. Before the devaluing of its offerings by a populist right. And before it was asked to reckon with its own investment in a status quo propped up by ongoing inequalities.

The promise is partly, then, that one can continue with how life used to feel before everything became too intensely political. This promise of not being affected coexists with a minimal optimism that the near-past will become the future again. Keir Starmer at the Labour Party conference in 2023 made a promise: 'Britain will get its future back.' The future to be retrieved looks a lot like the near-past. Part of the promise is stability and calm:

But they also look out at the chaos – in the world and at Westminster – and want to know can we find that elusive path to an economy that serves their community? Can we deliver the rock of stability they need to move forward in their lives? Shelter from the storm and a passage to calmer waters. Because conference, we should never forget that politics should tread lightly on peoples' lives. That our job is to shoulder the burden for working people, carry the load, not add to it. (Starmer, 2023)

But it is also a promise of a different present, one less dominated by tumult, the pressure of insecurity and an onrushing bad future. The vision of the future present is one in which the present will feel ... *freer*:

> Conference, we have to be a government that takes care of the big questions so working people have the freedom to enjoy what they love. More time, more energy, more possibility, more life.
>
> It could be football. Could be fishing. Or just quiet time with your family. But we all need that, conference. We all need the ability to look forward – to move forward – free from anxiety. That's what getting our future back really means. (Starmer, 2023)

Freedom is partly, here, about a different relation with the time of the present. The promised relation with the present is one based on enjoyment that also resonates with Fukuyama's phrase from 1992 – 'desire for comfortable self-preservation' – and contrasts markedly with the combination of urgency and catastrophe that characterises the impasse of progressivism.

'Getting the future back' is a phrase full of nostalgia for the near-past. The means for the return of the near-past in a different future present are familiar. A series of means are invoked – principally 'building' and 'growth' – that themselves recall the "long 90s" mixture of social liberalism and the market economy:

> And here's why. Because getting Britain building again is critical for economic growth. Our most important mission. Because it's also a means ... to soften that hard road. Deliver on national renewal. And escape the cost-of-living crisis permanently.
>
> That's why this Labour Party will fight the next election on economic growth. An economy that works for the whole country is what the British people want. (Starmer, 2023)

'Growth' and 'building' both imply a comfortable, mostly smooth return to the long-lost linear time of improvement. Lost to progressives, the future of progress is still just about available to liberals, given how close the near-past is. But in making the minimal optimism of progress just about available again, what is denied, implicitly, is the urgency of the present – the demand for some kind of structural change that would address racial and other injustices.

We hear a similar hope for progress again in Joe Biden's 2021 inauguration. Offered in the aftermath of the capital insurrection, amid COVID-19 and a war on truth, his promise is of a unity that restarts the future. As well as an impassioned attachment to America and the American dream, the means are the liberal virtues of a 'little tolerance and humility' and the figure of light touch sociality 'the neighbour':

We can see each other not as adversaries but as neighbours. We can treat each other with dignity and respect. We can join forces, stop the shouting and lower the temperature. For without unity there is no peace, only bitterness and fury, no progress, only exhausting outrage. No nation, only a state of chaos. This is our historic moment of crisis and challenge. And unity is the path forward. And we must meet this moment as the United States of America. (Biden, 2021)

The crisis is, in part, but not exclusively, a crisis of how the present feels. As with Starmer, the present and future is one of precariousness. As Biden (2021) goes on, 'Look, I understand that many of my fellow Americans view the future with fear and trepidation. I understand they worry about their jobs. I understand like their dad they lay in bed at night staring at the ceiling thinking: "Can I keep my healthcare? Can I pay my mortgage?" ' To inaugurate a new future, America must return to the values of tolerance and the promise of the unified nation. For Biden, the call and promise is that 'We must end this uncivil war that pits red against blue, rural versus urban, conservative versus liberal.' Lowering the 'temperature' is key.

The content of the promises is recognisable, fusing residual social democratic promises wrapped up in the nation as a community of support with the virtues of social liberalism and the continued operation of the market economy. Again, the promises are themselves a return. Optimistically, the promise is that you will be able to hope again that the future will once again be better than the present. No one is offering a guarantee of what the future will be (there are too many anti-liberal forces still at work which both Starmer and Biden name) but what is offered is a kind of weak or minimal hope. A hope for life without disruption, other than the welcome change of being able to cast aside the too much bad intensity of the present. A hope that you will be able to feel a good future again, without having to change or confront anything you don't want to. A hope that you won't have to change your life too much, that you won't have to reckon with inequalities or confront your own complicity. The promise is that you can look away again from what inflames the present – no more horror or guilt at genocide, no more "white tears" at racism, no more having to face what is revealed when liberalism's veneer is ripped off and its promises are troubled. The progressive left – with its call to centre race in the eye of the present's storm – is as much responsible for the inflamed present as right-wing populists on this account. Both confront liberalism with what lies beneath its stories of triumph.

Liberalism's promise is, then, of a twofold return to how the present used to feel, for those for whom the present used to be relatively comfortable. If you wish, you don't need to be affected by politics anymore. You can be bored, and you can detach and turn away again. You can be affected by something better than the tumult of the present, now that the "temperature" will have been lowered. And as you detach, you can weakly attach to the comforting hopes for the future that once felt just about in reach. "Growth" will return, bringing with it a sustainable future not only for you, but also for your loved ones. "Building" will happen. Uniting the offer of detachment, and the promise of hope for the return of normality again, is another hope: that in truth, nothing ever need change. The unfortunate turbulence of the present is a temporary aberration rather than structural condition. Become liberal again and we can all return to the better non-crisis near-past.

Conclusion: The Promise of Disappearance

Feeling nothing apart from the comforting presence of an incrementally better future once again on the horizon is the feeling of history ending again, releasing the world from its propulsion. It is the feeling of detaching not only from a resurgent white supremacy that finds its home in right-wing populism but also from progressive demands that whiteness be confronted, and that racial and other inequalities be addressed in the present to bring about a better future. Liberalism as a structure of feeling oscillates between outbursts of the defensive bellicosity that has always lurked within it and a minimal hope that the present is an aberration, that already comfortable subjects can return unblemished to a good near-past. Wrapped up in melancholy, confounded and made defensive by the lack of love for its "good objects", liberalism promises the tamping down of political feelings (including liberalism's own). Soon, you will be able to withdraw again from not only from a present overfull with demagogues and disturbing demands for justice but from having to think or feel about politics at all, including liberalism! Liberalism aspires to a future where it no longer needs to be consciously felt or defended – as the normality of ever-ongoing progress returns, and the antagonistic present is retrospectively revealed to be an unfortunate aberration.

Perhaps once, liberalism's tone was a simpler one. Passion for equality before the law and the rights of the individual coexisted with a more-or-less disguised racial superiority over a range of others who were to be improved, saved or civilised. But the crisis of liberalism is an affective one, as much as it is a crisis of the institutions, rationalities, and practices that compose liberalism. The contradictions are everywhere in a structure of feeling haunted by the shock of rejection, unsettled by the progressive claim that injustices are foundational to liberalism rather than its unfinished business, and the desperate hope of return to a near-past that is chronologically close and yet affectively distant. Liberal melancholia papers over the bleak possibility that there are no longer any good objects. Bellicosity erupts alongside calls for dialogue. Paranoia and the obsession with specific figures sit uncomfortably with charging others with the crimes of unreason.

Liberalism's affective confusion is a symptom of the problem of how to account for the dangerous, and bewildering, lack of love for liberalism. By promising the disappearance of politics, and its own erasure back into the comfort of common sense, the promise is also that change need not happen. Rupture, and the opening up of alternatives, are aberrations rather than necessities. Events such as Brexit or the election of Trump were associated with the dangerous forces of irrationality and unreason. The hopes that animate them are dismissed as manipulative lies or, at best, substitutions. The demands of movements like Black Lives Matter are too much for a liberalism that desires to disappear; they appear as unreasonable rejections of a liberalism that can still offer opportunity. Rejecting the lure of a break with the present, the kind of negative hope founded in rupture, liberalism reasserts not only its own rightness but also the promise of the end of history. The subjects of liberalism can continue to attach to the weak promise that their future will be better (though not dramatically different) than the present. Nothing need change – except that strident demands for change return to the side lines of liberalism's placid rein. Liberal democracy need not be the stakes of politics. It can instead return to being its unseen ground, if only we can bring back the near-past and the comforting assurance of history's in-built progress towards quietude.

5
Conclusion: Into the Moving Present

Introduction: The Cracking of "There Is No Alternative"

A few days after a failed assassination attempt, Donald Trump prepared to accept the Republication nomination for president at the 2024 Republican National Convention. He was preceded on the convention's final night by a performance of *American Bad Ass* by Kid Rock, an introduction from UFC's Dana White, and an endorsement from Terry Boella, performing as his famous character "Hulk Hogan", the retired world wrestling federation star who was integral to the worldwide popularity of what is reportedly Trump's favourite "sport". Speaking of the assassination attempt in ever more animated, agitated terms, Hogan first took off his jacket, and then melodramatically ripped his T-shirt in half to reveal a red vest with the slogan "Trump-Vance". The crowd's cheers grew in intensity before Hogan finished by shouting the phrase that enacts right-wing populisms' time-loop optimism: 'What happened last week, when they took a shot at my hero. And they tried to kill the next president of the United States, enough was enough. And I said, Let Trumpamania run wild brother, let Trumpamania rule again, let Trumpamania make America Great Again' (Hogan, 2024).

In Trump's acceptance speech the tone darkened, although the intensity of the crowd remained. Alongside his customary jokes, claims about inflation, and lies about the stolen 2020 election, Trump pivoted from a message of unity to once again invoke the grave threat posed to America by the 'massive invasion on the southern border' (Trump, 2024c). The mostly white audience in the convention hall held up signs: 'Mass Deportation Now!'. The 'Now' was in red, urgently punctuated.

Two days before in the UK, a different tone had been promised. Keir Starmer's briefing notes for the first King's Speech of his new government performed a return of liberalism's moderation. Promising 'stability' and 'growth' in order to 'fix the foundations of this nation for the long term' and enable 'national renewal', he claimed that his agenda would bring an end to the performative and divisive politics of the present: 'The snake oil charm of populism may sound seductive, but it drives us into the dead end of further division and greater disappointment', he claimed (Starmer, 2024; Crerar, 2024b).

An ageing wrestler ripping off his shirt before the cheers of a crowd and a UK prime minister promising to counter 'snake oil charm' are both symptoms of the conjunctural crisis into which we have written *The Politics of Feeling*. As we write this conclusion in the interim between the UK and the US 2024 elections, the present is tense and the future uncertain. Our times have a texture of their own, quickened and dispersed through the digital, the churn of the feed. Fragments of the unfolding present circulate as an image, a clip, a meme, and a reaction. Flags wave, faces contort. Leaders pump their fists or wave serenely to the picture-snapping crowd. Someone stumbles. A bullet path appears. What happened, what is happening, and what is going to happen next are matters of dispute. And no one yet knows how thoroughly AI will dissolve what little certainty we can yet muster about what appears before us on our algorithmically curated screens – or what will happen then.

The present unfolds a multiplicity of ways of feeling politically, of investing with urgency and significance a present moment that might otherwise feel stuck or suspended. The cracking of neoliberal common sense post 2008 has created both an impasse and an opening. "There is no alternative" was one way in which neoliberal hegemony was achieved in the 1980s in both the US and the UK, and part of the answer to the puzzle of why the changes this book documents did not happen immediately after the 2008 financial crisis, despite the presence of multiple forms of discontent and the already waning promissory legitimacy of neoliberal ideas, ideals, policies, and programmes. But "there is no alternative" was always more fragile than it appeared, based as it was on forms of resignation and acquiescence and the absence of positive attachment (Gilbert, 2015). All it takes is for a part of that complex to change for neoliberal common sense to become something else. What happens when frustration and irritation become anger, for example? Or if grudging acquiescence shifts to explicit rejection, even in the absence of the positive proposal of alternatives? Our premise has been that populism, progressivism, and a newly bellicose liberalism at once reflect and generate such shifts in feeling and orientation.

The cracking and breaking of "there is no alternative" is sign and symptom of the conjunctural crisis we detailed in the introduction playing out on the affect-imbued, ideological, and hegemonic levels. Partly this falling apart is expressed in the new public politics of turbulence and intensity that cycles through scenes such as Hogan's stunt, the call for deportation, and Starmer's promise of not feeling again. As we have argued throughout this book, the present conjunctural crisis has been marked by the ratcheting up of intensity, with judgments of whose intensity is wrong or too much depending on political position. We have seen the fast emergence of new cleavages – between Trump supporters and never-Trump republicans, between Brexit and Remain supporters, between centrist democrats or Labour supporters and the Sanders or Corbyn left, and so on. Beyond the realm of formal politics, anger and rage circulate both in movements that call urgently for justice, recalling the liberatory politics of passionate intensity, and in racist and misogynist backlashes to those same calls for justice, and their challenges to structural inequality. Minorities become subject to a nihilistic politics of ressentiment, with rage moving quickly and erratically between different mediated targets, most recently trans people and people seeking asylum. Division and discord agitate the present. Political feeling overheats, collapses. In keeping with Gilbert and Fisher's emphasis on disaffection, we can find in amidst the maelstrom a certain 'numbness' (Gilbert 2015: 33). This is, we have argued, part of how structures of feeling create difference both between and within the multiple structures of feeling of our affective present. The intensity available to some is bound up with the alienation and disaffection of others.

This conflictual, uneasy politics of (un)feeling is a symptom of the crisis that takes hold as "there is no alternative" breaks down. It is moot whether all this amounts to the revival of the capacity to imagine a '*coherent* alternative', as Fisher (2009, emphasis added) puts it in his definition of capitalist realism, or a '*viable* alternative', in Gilbert's (2015, emphasis added) terms. So many of the ring-wing populist figures and events that are most associated with the turbulence of the present are characterised by the indeterminacy of their relationship with neoliberalism. Do they reject or reproduce its premises? Or both? Or neither? Trump is at once "after" neoliberalism in his protectionist America First rhetoric and, at the same time, the exemplar of neoliberal individualism taken to its limit. From performing the role of the sovereign who decides in *The Apprentice* to his refusal to ever apologise, his is an individualism without constraint. As Brown puts it, Trump performs a 'desublimated will to power' (Brown, 2019: 172). In the UK, Brexit harboured contradictory fantasies of the UK as a deregulated "Singapore-on-the-Thames" and a return to a British nationalist past of sovereign control. More money for the NHS was juxtaposed with new trade deals in a newly confident nation "freed" to globalise outside of the shackles of the EU. An exit from neoliberalism and more neoliberalism were promised to result from the same destabilising, disruptive events.

Brexit and the 2016 and now 2024 election of Trump at once broke with, reproduced, started again, maintained, and ruptured the complex that is neoliberalism. Amidst this indeterminacy, what felt certain was that the common sense of no alternative had burst open. Like an understory now exposed to full sun, populism, and progressivism flourish in the opening, bringing with them tones and atmospheres – the anger of the left behind, the outrage of the too online, the emergency-animated urgency of progressivists – that are very different from the shrug of grudging resignation that was the dominant gestural expression of "there is no alternative". Liberalism attempts to feel its way back – but increasingly embattled, it finds itself in the weeds. No longer beholden to the inevitability of the status quo, the present feels at once stuck and overly eventful. And the future is up for grabs.

Feeling for the (a) Future

In this conjunctural crisis, populism, progressivism, and liberalism emerge as alternate ways of feeling and experiencing the present, investing the past, and projecting a future. Structures of feeling are not only feelings unfolding in the present, but feelings *about* the present. Are we inhabiting a moment of rupture and renewal (populism)? Or is the present a time of urgent action to complete our historical destiny and avert disaster (progressivism)? Or is this all an unfortunate detour that we can hope to forget (liberalism)? These feelings about the present are also ways of attaching to or detaching from the past – whether as a long arc of progress, a history of barbarism, or a repository of idealised moments to be recovered. And most of all, feeling in and of the present holds out a promise for the future: that it can be good again (even great!), that we can avoid the worst (happening again, happening to "us"), or that the old promises still abide.

Our propositions trace out how structures of feeling intensify or anaesthetise the present by organising attachments to both the past and the future. As our propositions on populism suggest, right-wing populism solves the problem of the end of the future by holding out the optimistic possibility that, in the future, things will be great again. This great future will be made in the image of an almost-lost, idealised past (of unquestioned masculinity and white upward mobility), now recuperated from the demand for "improvement" that both liberalism and progressivism seem to have foisted upon it. The excesses that are so central to right-wing populism, including the registers of fun and bellicose anger that Hulk Hogan's convention performance invoked, enact affectively the necessary disruptive break with the near-past of liberal common sense that is the condition for the return of the good past of blameless privilege. Present-day precariousness is blamed on the "establishment", the "elite", or migrants and racialised groups who are seen as having taken or received unearned recognition. These usurpers must be violently excluded and expelled if the good past is to return in the future. The temporality of right-wing populism is both a loop and a break: a return to greatness in a new illiberal future.

Conclusion

The progressive structure of feeling also responds to the loss of the future, but differently. The crisis of the present and the shadow that has fallen over the future means that progressivism has lost its defining object: its sense of history as a journey of continuous progress towards the "good society". With the disturbing realisation that what once passed for "progress" was fossil fuelled and built on the destruction of worlds, progressivism (unlike right-wing populism) cannot alight on an unconditionally good past – except perhaps one buried irretrievably in the pre-modern and pre-colonial age. But the past does offer something. It shimmers with fragments of freedom dreams not quite fulfilled, moments of action and solidarity that still transmit hope. The progressive structure of feeling revitalises the present by resurrecting attachment to these moments, infusing them into an exhausted present. Everything is immediately consequential because the bad future unfolding from the bad past must (and can) be averted. This paradoxical recovery of progress after the end of the future gives progressivism its vitality today and allows it to offer a new passionate intensity in the present.

Liberalism, buffeted by all this intensity, finds its own temporal solutions to the impasse. Unable to locate the objects that would ignite a passionate love for liberalism, it can only offer the weak hope of ending this detour into a too intense present by once again exiting the political and ending history. Despairing of the turbulent times, liberalism (like populism) attaches its hope to the restoration of the past in the future. While populism's "great" past is non-specific and idealised, liberalism's promised future is a return to the near past and a lost telos. Liberalism waves again its final offer: a future of no more history, no more ideology, only the clear, invisible water of liberal common sense, flowing inexorably through a series of imperfect (but well intentioned) presents towards a better future.

In a conjunctural crisis, the range of possibilities expands. What had been taken for granted no longer holds. New lines of discord and alternatives emerge. Feeling around in a constantly receding present, we find that even the rhythm of time has become differentiated: impassive or explosive, turning back or hurtling forward. Time loops, it breaks, it detours. The past, present, and the future are invested with possibilities of redemption, recovery. For things to be different than they were and also different than they are becoming.

Structures of Feeling Differently

Our propositions have attempted to orientate us to this crowd of structures of feeling through which the conjunctural crisis is made and felt. As the appeal or hold of ideas weakens, the range of possibilities expands, and what was once accepted as common sense is questioned. We may in this sense be "after ideology", but this does not mean that programmatic politics no longer exists or that there is no difference in the ideas and practical actions undertaken by Republicans or Democrats, the Conservative or Labour Party, let alone other political parties. Instead, when we point to the rise of the politics of feeling, we reflect upon how, in our digitally mediated times, it is *not only* our ideas, beliefs, and commitments that address the issues of our day. We "address" them also with our feelings – with how we attach and detach, become swept up or left cold.

Such a politics of feeling is neither purely individual nor mechanically given by "position", whether class position or other intersectional identities. That is, who we are and where we stand in relation to the conditions of our lives does matter; it affects not only our material interests but the availability and attraction of certain feelings and orientations. And yet our positionality does not determine our political feelings, not least because there are a multitude of mobile and overlapping structures of feeling continuously unfolding in our post-common-sense present. There are alternatives. Patterns or differentiations of feeling are constantly unfolding, pinging off the latest event or scene, taking form in the reactions and reactions to the reactions (Davies, 2023). It is not just that our differences are reflected in how we (are able to) feel but also *how we feel actively differentiates* the political field, distributing intensity, and disaffection in ways that both distinguish political formations and create them.

Structures of feeling are imbued with relations of power and domination that exceed them. While sometimes they gain strength from how they subvert and challenge these relations (for example, consider the class politics that inheres in excessive enjoyment of "owning the [university educated] libs"), they may also provide ballast to relations of domination. We see this in how all three structures of feeling centre and elevate *white* feelings – whether of woundedness (populism), guilt and heroism (progressivism), or presumed universality (liberalism). We also note how these structures of feeling are contorted around the hetero-normativity and masculinism of public discourse; this is most obvious in the case of right-wing populism, but it is there too in what gets silenced by the submerged promise of progressive time and in liberalism's call for trusting quietude.

This doesn't mean that they don't also course with minoritarian feelings and resistance. Even when feelings are collective, they are never uniform or all-encompassing. For this reason, we have mostly avoided saying things like "populists", "progressives", or "liberals", and *The Politics of Feeling* is not an explanation for why individuals or groups vote as they do in any given election, although we hope it offers some clues. Rather, we have been talking about tendencies, currents, and available ways of feeling. Individuals may find themselves allured or repelled, swept up or turned off – or vacillating between these possibilities from one moment to the next. Whatever appears consistent is continually being challenged, undone, and reconfigured by the minor feelings that fall out of the dominant mood. These minor feelings may surface in signs of disaffection, refusal, or retreat. But there is also the potential for minor feelings to coalesce into a transformative surge of newly collective intensity that shakes the present loose and shifts its coordinates. Structures of feeling are not determinate. They are open, evolving, always escaping our grasp.

We recognise that in offering a critique of the feeling-structures of contemporary political formations, we have tread on tender ground and risked being misinterpreted – a chance one always takes when writing but one that may be intensified by the problem that nobody likes to have their feelings "critiqued". Focussing on political adversaries' emotions is a classic way to discredit them, whether by calling them "snowflakes" or by implying that they have been emotionally manipulated and "whipped up" by manipulative leaders. By talking about the politics of feeling, at times our analysis might veer into the lane of such attacks (we hope not). Moreover, it is still the case that to be called emotional, especially when it comes to public matters, is redolent of the exclusion of women and racialised, sexualised and classed others from the "public sphere" of Western political theory. The mere idea that politics involves feelings may be considered an announcement of its degradation. It is possible that some will interpret *The Politics of Feeling* as being a condemnation of (others') feelings, while others will read it as an endorsement of a "post-truth" era. Neither of these reflects our intent.

What distinguishes our project from either a condemnation or celebration of political feelings is that we do not consider feelings to be something "other" to politics or to "truth". Our premise is that politics unfolds (not just now, but also historically) in the more-or-less consistent patterns of relations between feelings, attachments, and tendencies that are then recognised as political formations (e.g. populist, progressive, liberal). What has changed is not *the presence of* feelings in politics but their centrality to political antagonism today. And we contend that what has thrust the politics of feeling into the limelight (and led to the 21st century rise of populism and progressivism as political orientations without "ideology" per se) is the cracking of neoliberal common sense under the strain of a conjunctural crisis marked (in both the UK and the US, though differently) by economic and political insecurity, reduced prospects for working and lower-middle classes, and the collapse of faith in national trajectories. (One only needs to make America or Britain great again on the premise that the direction of travel has been otherwise.) Further, the rise of a politics of feeling has happened together with the acceleration of circulation and "reaction" in our era of intensified digital mediation. In this conjuncture, we have entered a period of active contest between antagonistic political formations that, as we have just argued, provide alternative ways to feel not only about the crises of living unfolding before us today, but also about our differentiated pasts and our shared futures.

Our aim with this book has been to produce a sense of this moving present, of its trajectories and blockages, its pressure points, and the cross-cutting currents of our shared but differentiated times. The propositional mode has allowed us to put forward interpretations of populism, progressivism, and liberalism without pretending that these are exhaustive or definitive. As we said in the introduction, they are offered to spark discussion, and in the hope and expectation of disagreement. The propositions are essays, attempts to see what we can capture and name in the ever-receding moment of lived experience. By venturing to critique what is in fact in motion, we hope that we might create new possibilities, such as the potential to think and feel across the three political formations as well as to recognise the strands of minor politics that weave through them. The hope of *The Politics of Feeling* is to have provided some partial insight into the affective present in its contingency, its momentariness.

Afterword: In the Impasse

We write this afterword the day after the 2024 re-election of Donald J. Trump for a second presidential term. We write through a mixture of sadness, anger, and irritation, but little shock. We write from within the affective turbulence that marks the day after what, from within the pull to attach and detach from the maelstrom of this moment, feels like the beginning of a resolution to this conjunctural crisis, but we hope may extend the impasse as it generates its own counter-reaction. We write as a now familiar cycle of progressive and liberal recrimination begins to gather in intensity, as consoling, but contradictory, explanations are offered and vehemently rejected as being themselves part of the problem, as catastrophic futures proliferate, in ways that make it hard to discern quite what the real danger is, and as the alarm sounds about how the UK might echo America in the aftermath of the election of another right wing populist, Kemi Badenoch, as leader of the Conservative Party. But we also write amid jubilation and time-loop and other optimisms, vengeful and other joys, relief, or even ecstasy (as well as numbness and other detachments that still characterise so many people's ways of relating to politics). However we ourselves feel, we try to hold onto a recognition of the multiplicity and differentiation that is currently unfolding across the political-affective field. Amid all this feeling, someone repeats the desperate, almost last hope of liberalism as its crisis threatens, once again, to become terminal – feeling less. 'Something I hope we can do no matter who you voted for', Joe Biden says as he promises a return to the low intensity normality of an "orderly transition of power", 'is see each other not as adversaries but as fellow Americans, bring down the temperature' (Mason, 2024).

The revisions for this book were due days after the presidential election. For the most part, we resisted the lure to introduce new material into the book in light of the event. We'll leave it for the reader to decide how our propositions might relate to this and other emergent events, what they might help us notice, and what they might miss or misrecognise. In the days leading up to the election, amid our trepidation, uncertainty, and glimmers of a fragile hope, we were thinking together about how to respond to a common injunction across the reviewer comments on the draft manuscript – to shift from propositions to prescriptions, to set out what a good affective politics should do. In conversations and questions after talks on the book we've been asked versions of the question the reviewers, in their different ways, posed: what affective lures and appeals should the kind of politics we are committed to offer?

We understand the demand, indeed right now it feels even more urgent, and can feel various desires gathered within it: to have guardrails amidst all this uncertainty, to offer a ground for hope, to identify what should be done after other strategies have run aground, to simply perform commitment. We experimented with what we might advocate, wanting to take responsibility. Perhaps, we could gather elements from each of the different structures of feeling, advocating for new arrangements. One can imagine the propositions changing and recombining to make possible the emergence of new possibilities. What if the left was excessive, dressing up as garbage contractors, driving forklift trucks through polystyrene walls, being introduced by ageing wrestlers, unashamedly performing stunts? Perhaps we should affirm the allure of unfeeling, indeed decry all this feeling today and perform the fiction and fantasy that politics could ever be affect-free, or sound the alarm ever more intensely and advocate for the politics of panic. But every affirmation pulled us into an intimacy with political forms and feelings we either reject or harbour an ambivalence around. Perhaps, we needed to amplify traditions of thought and action on the radical left that inspire us and advocate for new, yet unnamed, affective lures and appeals – militant fun or panic optimism or tragic joy. We began to laugh at the absurdity of our inventions as we conjured ever stranger affective hybrids.

And as our laughter died down, we realised it hid another absurdity – of us telling other people how to feel, of issuing proclamations for the left from our position. Others are better placed to do that work. But in that moment, we felt what we were committed to: the promise of the type of analysis we have performed in this book, a diagnostic critique that affirms a simple but oft forgotten lesson from Stuart Hall. Writing on Thatcherism in *The Great Moving Right Show* (2017: 174), he warns against the satisfactions of a consoling analysis, advocating, via Gramsci, for facing the 'present as it is'. *The Politics of Feeling* has a fidelity to this mode of sensing and understanding the present, in all its contradictions and paradoxes, in all its difficulty and discomfort, as different forces gather and disperse. We end, then, with one thing we are unambivalent about: the political necessity of analysis that takes seriously the affective lures and promises of today's political forms, practices an alertness and responsiveness to what might be happening, and thinks aloud, affirming its own contingency. We hope our propositions are useful, in some small, inevitably partial, way, to understanding and hopefully acting within this conjuncture, amid a crisis that we hope is not yet resolved.

References

Addley, Esther. 2019. 'Like a damp towel on a line': The day Boris Johnson got stuck on a zip wire. *The Guardian* 16 June 2019. Accessed 01 Oct 2024: www.theguardian.com/politics/2019/jul/16/stuck-zip-wire-boris-johnson-london-2012-olympics

Ahmed, Sara. 2010. *The Promise of Happiness*. Duke University Press.

Ahmed, Sara. 2024. *Feminist Killjoys*. Penguin.

Ahmann, Chloe. 2024. *Futures After Progress: Hope and Doubt in Late Industrial Baltimore*. The University of Chicago Press.

Akkerman, Agnes, Muddle, Cas, and Zaslove, Andrej. 2014. How populist are the people? Measuring populist attitudes in voters. *Comparative Political Studies* 47(9): 1324-1353.

Alderman, Naomi. 2016. *The Power*. Little, Brown, and Company.

Anderson, Amanda. 2000. *The Powers of Distance: Cosmopolitanism and the Cultivation of Detachment*. Princeton University Press.

Anderson, Ben. 2021. Affect and critique: A politics of boredom. *Environment and Planning D: Society and Space* 39(2): 197-217.

Anderson, Ben. 2010. Preemption, precaution, preparedness: Anticipatory action and future geographies. *Progress in Human Geography* 34(6): 777-798.

Anderson, Ben. 2014. *Encountering Affect: Capacities, Apparatuses, Conditions*. Routledge.

Anderson, Ben. 2023. Forms and scenes of attachment: A cultural geography of promises. *Dialogues in Human Geography* 13(3): 392-409.

Anderson, Ben, Wilson, Helen F., Forman, Peter G., Heslop, Julia, Ormerond, Emma, and Maestri, Gaja. 2020. Brexit: Modes of uncertainty and futures in an impasse. *Transactions of the Institute of British Geographers* 45(2): 256-269.

Anker, Elisabeth Robin. 2014. *Orgies of Feeling: Melodrama and the Politics of Freedom*. Duke University Press.

Applebaum, Anne. 2021. *Twilight of Democracy: The Seductive Lure of Authoritarianism.* Vintage.

Atwood, Margaret. 1985. *The Handmaid's Tale.* Harper Collins.

Atwood, Margaret. 2022. I invented Gilead. The Supreme Court is making it real. *The Atlantic* 13 May 2022. Accessed 01 Oct 2024: www.theatlantic.com/ideas/archive/2022/05/supreme-court-roe-handmaids-tale-abortion-margaret-atwood/629833/

Avalos, Lisa. 2023. The under-enforcement of crimes against black women. *Case Western Reserve Law Review*, https://digitalcommons.law.lsu.edu/faculty_scholarship/458

Baldwin, Andrew. 2022. *The Other of Climate Change: Racial Futurism, Migration, Humanism.* Rowman & Littlefield.

Ball, James. 2017. *Post-Truth: How Bullshit Conquered the World.* Biteback Publishing.

Baspehlivan, Uygar. 2024. Cucktales: Race, sex and enjoyment in the reactionary memescape. *International Political Sociology* 18(3): olae026.

Beckert, Jens. 2020. The exhausted futures of neoliberalism: From promissory legitimacy to social anomy. *Journal of Cultural Economy* 13(3): 318–330.

Bell, Daniel. 1962. *The End of Ideology: On the Exhaustion of Political Ideas in the Fifties.* Harvard University Press.

Benjamin, Walter. 1968. *Illuminations.* Harcourt, Brace and World.

Benjamin, Walter. 1994. Left-wing melancholy. In *The Weimar Republic Sourcebook*, ed. Anton Kaes, Martin Jay, and Edward Dimendberg, 304–306. University of California Press.

Berardi, Franco. 2011. *After the Future.* AK Press.

Berlant, Lauren. 2011. *Cruel Optimism.* Duke University Press.

Berlant, Lauren and Stewart, Kathleen. 2019. *The Hundreds.* Duke University Press.

Berry, Jeffrey M. and Sobieraj, Sarah. 2016. *The Outrage Industry: Political Opinion Media and the New Incivility.* Oxford University Press.

Biden, Joe. 2021. Full transcript of Joe Biden's inauguration speech. *BBC News* 20 January 2021. Accessed 01 Oct 2024: www.bbc.co.uk/news/world-us-canada-55656824

Blaazer, David. 2014. Progressivism: An idea whose time has gone? *Political Studies Review* 12(1): 6–16.

Blake, Aaron. 2016. The Trump response to Clinton's 'basket of deplorables' comment was quite good. *The Washington Post* 12 September 2016. Accessed 01 Oct 2024: www.washingtonpost.com/news/the-fix/wp/2016/09/12/trumps-initial-response-to-clintons-basket-of-deplorables-comment-was-a-very-good-one/

Blewett, Sam. 2024. Liz Truss' journey from Downing Street to 'deep state' conspiracist. *Politico* 12 March 2024. Accessed 01 Oct 2024: www.politico.eu/article/liz-truss-unlikely-journey-from-downing-street-chief-to-deep-state-conspiracist/

Block, Elena and Negrine, Ralph M. 2017. The populist communication style: Toward a critical framework. *International Journal of Communication* 11: 178–197.

Blyth, Mark. 2013. *Austerity: The History of a Dangerous Idea*. Oxford University Press.

Bogaards, Matthijs. 2017. Lessons from Brexit and Trump: populism is what happens when political parties lose control. *Zeitschrift für Vergleichende Politikwissenschaft* 11(4): 513–518.

Bosworth, Kai. 2019. The people know best: Situating the counter-expertise of populist pipeline opposition movements. *Annals of the American Association of Geographers* 109(2): 581–592.

Bosworth, Kai. 2022. The bad environmentalism of 'nature is healing' memes. *Cultural Geographies* 29(3): 353–374.

Bradley, Rizvanna. 2023. Too think love, or bearing the unbearable. In *The Affect Theory Reader 2: Worldings, Tensions, Futures*, ed. Gregory J. Seigworth and Carolyn Pedwell, 191–213. Duke University Press.

Brown, Wendy. 2000. Resisting left melancholia. In *Without Guarantees: In Honour of Stuart Hall*, ed. Paul Gilroy, Lawrence Grossberg, and McRobbie, Angela, 21–29. Verso.

Brown Wendy. 2019. *In the Ruins of Neoliberalism: The Rise of Antidemocratic Politics in the West*. Columbia University Press.

Cassidy, John. 2018. How Donald Trump became the author of his own 'Astonishingly Excellent' health. *The New Yorker* 2 May 2018. Accessed 01 Oct 2024: www.newyorker.com/news/our-columnists/how-donald-trump-became-the-author-of-his-own-astonishingly-excellent-health

Chait, John. 2017. Trump is failing at policy, but winning his race wars. *New York Magazine* 4 April 2017. Accessed 01 Oct 2024: https://nymag.com/intelligencer/2017/04/trump-is-failing-at-policy-but-winning-his-race-wars.html

Chun, Wendy Hui Kyong. 2017. *Updating to Remain the Same: Habitual New Media*. MIT Press.

Clarke, John. 2023. *The Battle for Britain: Crises, Conflicts and the Conjuncture*. Bristol University Press.

Closs-Stephens, Angharad. 2022. *National Affects: The Everyday Atmospheres of Being Political*. Bloomsbury.

Cockayne, Daniel. 2016. Entrepreneurial affect: Attachment to work practice in San Francisco's digital media sector. *Environment and Planning D: Society and Space* 34(3): 456–473.

Colebrook, Claire. 2023. *Who Would You Kill to Save the World?* University of Nebraska Press.

Coleman, Rebecca. 2018. Theorizing the present: digital media, pre-emergence and infra-structures of feeling. *Cultural Studies* 32(4): 600–622.

Coleman, Rebecca. 2020. Refresh: On the temporalities of digital media 'Re's. *Media Theory* 4(2): 55–84.

Corbyn, Jeremy. 2018. We're rebuilding Britain – video. *Labour.org* 27 September 2018. Accessed 01 Oct 2024: www.youtube.com/watch?v=bpCRQZiQ6Y8

Coughlan, Sean. 2016. Tony Blair warns of 'flabby liberalism'. *BBC News* 22 March 2016. Accessed 01 Oct 2024: www.bbc.co.uk/news/education-35862598

Cox, Michael. 2017. The rise of populism and the crisis of globalisation: Brexit, Trump and beyond. *Irish Studies in International Affairs* 28(1): 9–17.

Crace, John. 2024. Sunak and Starmer wrap up their final debate of despair. *The Guardian* 26 June 2024. Accessed 01 Oct 2024: www.theguardian.com/politics/article/2024/jun/26/sunak-and-starmer-wrap-up-their-final-debate-of-despair

References

Crerar, Pippa. 2024a. Tony Blair urges Starmer to keep grip on immigration to tackle rise of far right. *The Guardian* 9 July 2024. Accessed 01 Oct 2024: www.theguardian.com/politics/article/2024/jul/09/tony-blair-keir-starmer-labour-immigration-far-right

Crerar, Pippa. 2024b. Starmer counts on promises he can fulfil to rebuild voters' trust. *The Guardian* 17 July 2024. Accessed 01 Oct 2024: www.theguardian.com/politics/article/2024/jul/17/starmer-counts-on-promises-he-can-fulfil-to-rebuild-voters-trust

D'Ancona, Matthew. 2017. *Post-truth: The New War on Truth and How to Fight Back*. Random House.

Darling, Jonathan. 2022. *Systems of Suffering*. Pluto.

Davidson, Mark and Ward, Kevin. 2024. Conjunctural urban geographies: Modes, methods, and meso-level concepts. *Progress in Human Geography*, Online early: https://doi.org/10.1177/03091325241251839

Davies, William. 2020. *This Is Not Normal: The Collapse of Liberal Britain*. Verso.

Davies, William. 2023. The reaction economy. *London Review of Books* 2 March 2023: 3–8.

Davis, Evan. 2017. *Post-Truth: Why We Have Reached Peak Bullshit and What We Can Do About It*. Little, Brown.

De Genova, Nicholas. 2018. Rebordering "the people": Notes on theorizing populism. *South Atlantic Quarterly* 117(2): 357–374.

Deneen, Patrick. 2018. *Why Liberalism Failed*. Yale University Press.

Derrida, Jacques. 1998. *Resistances of Psychoanalysis*. Stanford University Press.

Dunt, Ian. 2020. *How to Be a Liberal: The Story of Freedom and the Fight for Its Survival*. Canbury Press.

Edelman, Lee. 2004. *No Future: Queer Theory and the Death Drive*. Duke University Press.

Editorial, The Times. 2023. Don't underestimate Sunak and Hunt's dullness dividend. *The Times* 12 March 2023. Accessed 01 Oct 2024: www.thetimes.com/uk/politics/article/dont-underestimate-sunak-and-hunts-dullness-dividend-chrthc3fx

Editorial Board, NYT. 2013. President Barack Obama. *The New York Times* 21 January 2013. Accessed 01 Oct 2024: www.nytimes.com/2013/01/22/opinion/president-obamas-second-inauguration.html

Editorial Board, NYT. 2016. A chance to reset the Republican race. *The New York Times* 31 January 2016. Accessed 01 Oct 2024: www.nytimes.com/2016/01/31/opinion/sunday/a-chance-to-reset-the-republican-race.html

El-Mohtar, Amal. 2017. March's Book Club Pick: 'The Power,' by Naomi Alderman. *The New York Times* 25 October 2017. Accessed 01 Oct 2024: www.nytimes.com/2017/10/25/books/review/naomi-alderman-power.html

Ellis, Emma Grey. 2019. *Handmaid's Tale* garb is the viral protest uniform of 2019. *Wired* 5 June 2019. Accessed 01 Oct 2024: www.wired.com/story/handmaids-tale-protest-garb/

Fandos, Nicholas. 2024. Ocasio-Cortez loses the democratic socialists' endorsement over Israel. *The New York Times* 11 July 2024. Accessed 01 Oct 2024: www.nytimes.com/2024/07/11/us/politics/aoc-dsa-endorsement.html

Farage, Nigel. 2016. Nigel Farage: 'This will be a victory for real people' – video. *The Guardian* 24 June 2016. Accessed 01 Oct 2024: www.theguardian.com/politics/video/2016/jun/24/nigel-farage-eu-referendum-this-victory-for-real-people-video

Farage, Nigel. 2024. Nigel Farage announces he will stand as an MP – video. *INews* 3 June 2024. Accessed 01 Oct 2024: www.youtube.com/watch?v=x31rUFpxmQU

Feher, Michel. 2018. *Rated Agency: Investee Politics in a Speculative Age*. Zone Books.

Fisher, Mark. 2009. *Capitalism Realism: Is There No Alternative?* Zero Books.

Fisher, Mark. 2014. *Ghosts of My Life: Writings on Depression, Hauntology and Lost Futures*. Zero Books.

Flegenheimer, Matt. 2020. What democracy scholars thought of Trump's bible photo op. *The New York Times* 2 June 2020. Accessed 01 Oct 2024: www.nytimes.com/2020/06/02/us/politics/trump-holds-bible-photo.html

Fleming, Peter. 2019. *The Worst Is Yet to Come*. Repeater Books.

Foucault, Michel. 2008. *The Birth of Biopolitics*. Trans. Burchell, G. and Davidson, A. Palgrave Macmillan.

References

Folkers, Andreas. 2021. Fossil modernity: The materiality of acceleration, slow violence, and ecological futures. *Time and Society* 30(2): 223–246.

Frank, Thomas. 2020. *The People, No: A Brief History of Anti-Populism*. Metropolitan Books.

Freeden, Michael. 2014. Progress and progressivism: Thoughts on an elusive term. *Political Studies Review* 12(1): 68–74.

Freud, Sigmund. 1953[1900]. *The Interpretation of Dreams*. Standard Edition. Hogarth Press.

Fukuyama, Francis. 1989. The end of history? *The National Interest* 16(Summer): 3–18.

Fukuyama, Francis. 1992. *The End of History and the Last Man*. Penguin.

Fukuyama, Francis. 2020. Liberalism and its discontents: The challenges from the left and the right. *American Purpose* 5 October 2020. Accessed 01 Oct 2024: www.americanpurpose.com/articles/liberalism-and-its-discontent/

Fukuyama, Francis. 2022a. *Liberalism and Its Discontents*. Profile Books.

Fukuyama, Francis. 2022b. Putin's war on the Liberal Order. *Financial Times* 4 March 2022. Accessed 01 Oct 2024: www.ft.com/content/d0331b51-5d0e-4132-9f97-c3f41c7d75b3

Fukuyama, Francis. 2022c. A country of their own: Liberalism needs the nation. *Foreign Affairs* May/June 2022. Accessed 01 Oct 2024: www.foreignaffairs.com/articles/ukraine/2022-04-01/francis-fukuyama-liberalism-country

Garber, Megan. 2023. The truth won't matter. *The Atlantic* 3 December 2023. Accessed 01 Oct 2024: www.theatlantic.com/magazine/archive/2024/01/trump-lies-2024-reelection-facts/676133/#

Gilbert, Jeremy. 2015. Disaffected consent: That post democratic feeling. *Soundings* 60(Summer): 29–41.

Gilbert, Jeremy. 2019. This conjuncture: For Stuart Hall. *New Formations* 96-97: 5–37.

Gilbert, Jeremy and Williams, Alex. 2022. *Hegemony Now: How Big Tech and Wall Stress Won the World (And How We Win It Back)*. Verso.

Gilbert, Sophie. 2024. Four more years of unchecked misogyny. *The Atlantic* January/February. Accessed 01 Oct 2024: www.theatlantic.com/magazine/archive/2024/01/trump-sexual-abuse-misogyny-women/676124/

Giles, Chris and Parker, George. 2022. UK public finances shift from 'moron premium' to 'dullness dividend'. *Financial Times* 26 October 2022. Accessed 01 Oct 2024: www.ft.com/content/1dc057df-2ef0-47fa-bd40-3f5d229b0cff

Gilroy, Paul. 2004. *After Empire: Melancholia or Convivial Culture?* Routledge.

Glynos, Jason and Stavrakakis, Yannis. 2008. Lacan and political subjectivity: Fantasy and enjoyment in psychoanalysis and political theory. *Subjectivity* 24(1): 256–274.

Gökarıksel, Banu, Neubert, Chris, and Smith, Sara. 2019. Demographic fever dreams: Fragile masculinity and population politics in the rise of the global right. *Signs: Journal of Women in Culture and Society* 44(3): 561–587.

Goodhart, David. 2017. *The Road to Somewhere: The Populist Revolt and the Future of Politics.* C Hurst & Co.

Gopnik, Adam. 2019. *A Thousand Small Sanities.* Basic Books.

Gorrie, Nayuka. 2018. The Handmaid's Tale is not dystopian for black women – it's real life. *Special Broadcasting Service* 23 May 2018. Accessed 01 Oct 2024: www.sbs.com.au/voices/article/the-handmaids-tale-is-not-dystopian-for-black-women-its-real-life/varievrre.

Gregg, Melissa. 2018. *Counterproductive: Time Management in the Knowledge Economy.* Duke University Press.

Grossberg, Lawrence. 2019. Cultural studies in search of a method, or looking for conjunctural analysis. *New Formations* 96–97: 38–68.

Grusin, Richard. 2010. *Premediation: Affect and Mediation after 9/11.* Palgrave.

Gusterson, Hugh. 2017. From Brexit to Trump: Anthropology and the rise of nationalist populism. *American Ethnologist* 44(2): 209–214.

Hall, Stuart. 2017. *Selected Political Writings: The Great Moving Right Show and Other Essays.* Lawrence and Wishart.

Hall, Stuart and Massey, Doreen. 2010. Interpreting the crisis. *Soundings* 44(Spring): 57–71.

Hall, Stuart. Critcher, Chas., Jefferson, Tony, Clarke, John, and Roberts, Brian. 2013. *Policing the Crisis: Mugging, the State and Law & Order.* Macmillan.

Hannah-Jones, Nikole. 2024. *The 1969 Project: A New American Origin Story.* Penguin.

References

Harlander, Thomas. 2016. Great news! In multiverse theory, there are infinite worlds where Donald Trump did not win the election. *Los Angeles Magazine* 9 November 2016. Accessed 01 Oct 2024: https://lamag.com/politics/great-news-multiverse-theory-infinite-worlds-donald-trump-not-win-election

Harris-Parry, Melissa. 2022. Black masculinity and the slap heard round the world. *WNYC Studios: The Takeaway* 29 March 2022. Accessed 01 Oct 2024: www.wnycstudios.org/podcasts/takeaway/segments/what-slap-revealed-about-black-masculinity

Hart, Gillian. 2024. Modalities of conjunctural analysis: 'Seeing the present differently' through global lenses. *Antipode* 56(1): 135–164.

Hartman, Saidiya. 2002. The time of slavery. *South Atlantic Quarterly* 101(4): 757–77.

Heitzman, Chris. 2022. *The Coming Woke Catastrophe*. Academica Press.

Highmore, Ben. 2017. *Cultural Feelings: Mood, Meditation and Cultural Politics*. Routledge.

Hillenbrand, Margaret. 2023. *On the Edge: Feeling Precarious in China*. Columbia University Press.

Hochschild, Arlie. 2016. *Strangers in Their Own Land*. The New Press.

Hogan, Hulk. 2024. Hulk Hogan calls Trump 'my hero' at RNC – video. *ABC News* 19 July 2024. Accessed 01 Oct 2024: www.youtube.com/watch?v=ico2_fk3dGc

Holladay, Holly and Classen, Chandler. 2021. The drip, drip, drip of dystopia: The Handmaid's Tale, temporal boundaries, and affective investment. *Feminist Media Studies* 21(3): 477–492.

Hong, Cathy Park. 2020. *Minor Feelings: A Reckoning on Race and the Asian Condition*. Profile Books.

Hong, Renyi. 2022. *Passionate Work: Endurance After the Good Life*. Duke University Press.

Hook, Derek. 2017. What is "enjoyment as a political factor"? *Political Psychology* 38(4): 605–620.

HoSang, Daniel M., and Lowndes, Joseph E. 2019. *Producers, Parasites, Patriots: Race and the New Right-wing Politics of Precarity*. University of Minnesota Press.

Hunt, Elle. 2016. What is fake news? How to spot it and what you can do to stop it. *The Guardian* 17 December 2016. Accessed 01 Oct 2024: https://www.theguardian.com/media/2016/dec/18/what-is-fake-news-pizzagate

Ibrahim, Habiba, and Ahad, Badia. 2022. Introduction: Black temporalities in times of crisis. *The South Atlantic Quarterly* 121(1): 1–10.

Insider Paper @TheInsiderPaper 2020. 4 November. *BREAKING VIDEO: Scenes from #Nevada, Clark County Election Center where Registrar of Voters is addressing the ballots that still needs to be counted. This man shows up yelling.* [Tweet] Twitter: https://twitter.com/TheInsiderPaper/status/1324107564108386309?s=20

Jessop, Bob. 2019. Authoritarian neoliberalism: Periodization and critique. *South Atlantic Quarterly* 118(2): 343–361.

Johnson, Boris. 2020a. COVID-19: Self-isolating Boris Johnson says he feels 'as fit as a butcher's dog' – video. *Sky News* Monday 16 November 2020. Accessed 01 Oct 2024: https://news.sky.com/video/covid-19-self-isolating-boris-johnson-says-he-feels-as-fit-as-a-butchers-dog-12133725

Johnson, Boris. 2020b. Keynote speech. Accessed 01 Oct 2024: www.conservatives.com/news/boris-johnson-read-the-prime-ministers-keynote-speech-in-full

Johnson, Boris. 2019. Victory speech. Accessed 01 Oct 2024: www.bbc.co.uk/news/election-2019-50777071

Johnston, Matt. 2023. *How Hitchens Can Save the Left: Rediscovering Fearless Liberalism in an Age of Counter-Enlightenment.* Pitchstone Publishing.

Jong-Fast, Molly. 2023. Can Joe Biden ride 'boring' to re-election? *Vanity Fair* 5 September 2023. Accessed 01 Oct 2024: www.vanityfair.com/news/2023/09/joe-biden-2024-election

Jutel, Olivier. 2018. American populism, Glenn Beck and affective media production. *International Journal of Cultural Studies* 21(4): 375–392.

Kant, Immanuel. 1784 [1963]. Idea for a universal history from a cosmopolitan point of view. Translation by Lewis White Beck. In *On History*, The Bobbs-Merrill Co.

Kaufman, Eric. 2024. *The Third Awokening: A 12-Point Plan for Rolling Back Progressive Extremism.* Bombardier.

Kelley, Robin. 2002. *Freedom Dreams: The Black Radical Imagination*. Beacon Press.

Kelliher, Diarmaid. 2015. The 1984–5 miners' strike and the spirit of solidarity. *Soundings: A Journal of Politics and Culture* 60(Summer): 118–129.

Kellner, Douglas. 2016. *American Nightmare: Donald Trump, Media Spectacle, and Authoritarian Populism*. Sense Publishers.

Khiabany, Gholam. 2017. Introduction. In *Liberalism in Neoliberal Times: Dimensions, Contradictions, Limits*, ed. Alejandro Abraham-Hamanoiel, Des Freedman, Gholam Khiabany, Kate Nash, and Julian Petley, 1-12. Goldsmiths University Press.

Klein, Naomi. 2023. *Doppelganger: A Trip Into the Mirror World*. Allen Lane the Penguin Press Ltd.

Kornbluh, Anna. 2024. *Immediacy, or The Style of Too Late Capitalism*. Verso.

Koselleck, Reinhart. 2006. Crisis. *Journal of the History of Ideas* 67(2): 357–400.

Lacan, Jaques. *Television*. 1990. W.W. Norton & Company.

Laclau, Ernesto. 2005. *On Populist Reason*. Verso.

Langevang, Thilde, Steedman, Robin, Alacovska, Anna, Resario, Rashida, Kilu, Rufai, Sanda, Mohammad-Aminu. 2022. 'The show must go on!': Hustling through the compounded precarity of Covid-19 in the creative industries. *Geoforum* 136(November): 142–152.

Latour, Bruno. 1988. The politics of explanation: An alternative. In *Knowledge and Reflexivity, New Frontiers in the Sociology of Knowledge*, ed. Steve Woolgar, 155–177. Sage.

Lawson, Neal. 2021. Here's how a progressive alliance would actually work. *The Guardian* 24 June 2021. Accessed 01 Oct 2024: www.theguardian.com/commentisfree/2021/jun/24/how-progressive-alliance-tory-britain

Leach, Melissa, MacGregor, Hayley, Scoones, Ian, and Wilkinson, Annie. 2021. Post-pandemic transformations: How and why COVID-19 requires us to rethink development. *World Development* 138: 105233.

Lemke, T. 2001. 'The birth of bio-politics': Michel Foucault's lecture at the Collège de France on neo-liberal governmentality. *Economy and Society* 30(2): 190–207.

Levin, David P. and Bowker, Matthew H. 2019. *The Destroyed World and the Guilty Self*. Phoenix Publishing House.

Levitin, Daniel. 2017. *Weaponized Lies: How to Think Critically in the Post-Truth Era*. Viking.

Lewis, Hannah, Dwyer, Peter, Hodkinson, Stuart, and Waite, Louse. 2015. Precarious lives: Migrants, work and forced labour in the Global North. *Progress in Human Geography* 39(5): 580–600.

Lewis, Sophie. 2017. Dreams of Gilead. *Blind Field Journal* 14 June 2017. Accessed 01 Oct 2024: https://blindfieldjournal.com/2017/06/14/dreams-of-gilead/

Liptak, Kevin. 2021. Trump's presidency ends with American carnage. *CNN* 6 January 2021. Accessed 01 Oct 2024: https://edition.cnn.com/2021/01/06/politics/donald-trump-capitol-mob/index.html

Littler, Jo. 2018. *Against Meritocracy: Culture, Power and Myths of Mobility*. Routledge.

Logan, Brian. 2006. Review: Robert Newman *The Guardian* 6 July 2006. Accessed 01 Oct 2024: www.theguardian.com/stage/2006/jul/06/comedy

Lorey, Isabell. 2015. *States of Insecurity: Government of the Precarious*. Verso.

Losurdo, Dominico. 2014. *Liberalism: A Counter-History*. Verso.

Luce, Edward. 2017. *The Retreat of Western Liberalism*. Little Brown.

Luce, Edward. 2020, Populism and the smouldering rage of American poverty. *Financial Times* 17 January 2020. Accessed 01 Oct 2024: www.ft.com/content/24bb69aa-3621-11ea-a6d3-9a26f8c3cba4

Luger, Jason. 2024. Affective authoritarianism as joyful 'oeuvre?' Godly subjects and suburban gladiators *Cultural Geographies*, Online first.

Mason, Jeff 2024. Biden urges Americans to 'Bring down the temperature' after Trump's US election win. *Reuters* 7 November 2024. Accessed 08 Nov 2024: https://www.reuters.com/world/us/biden-set-address-nation-after-trumps-decisive-us-election-win-2024-11-07/

Maher, Bill. 2022. Explaining jokes to idiots: Oscars edition. *Real Time with Bill Maher, HBO* 8 April 2022. Accessed 01 Oct 2024: www.youtube.com/watch?v=p-c2eUltH58

Malatino, Hal. 2022. *Side Affects: On Being Trans and Feeling Bad*. University of Minnesota Press.

References

Manning, Erin. 2016. *The Minor Gesture*. Duke University Press.

Mardell, Mark. 2016. What links Trump's victory and Brexit? *BBC News* 10 November 2016. Accessed 01 Oct 2024: www.bbc.co.uk/news/election-us-2016-37922961

Massumi, Brian. 2002. *Parables for the Virtual: Movement, Affect, Sensation*. Duke University Press.

Massumi, Brian. 2015. *Ontopower: War, Powers, and the State of Perception*. Duke University Press.

Matheson, Calum Lister. 2022. Liberal tears and the rogue's yarn of sadistic conservativism. *Rhetoric Society Quarterly* 52(4): 341–355.

Matias, Cheryl E. 2016. *Feeling White: Whiteness, Emotionality, and Education*. Springer.

McCormack, Derek. 2023. The elements of affect theories. In *The Affect Theory Reader 2: Worldings, Tensions, Futures*, ed. Gregory J. Seigworth and Carolyn Pedwell, 63–84. Duke University Press.

McNalley, David. 2006. *Another World Is Possible: Globalization and Anti-Capitalism*. AK Press.

Meehan, Katie and Strauss, Kendra (eds). 2015. *Precarious Worlds: Contested Geographies of Social Reproduction*. University of Georgia Press.

Michaelson, Jay. 2023. Boring is good: The moral case for Joe Biden. *Rolling Stone* 25 April 2023. Accessed 01 Oct 2024: www.rollingstone.com/politics/political-commentary/joe-biden-2024-donald-trump-boring-important-1234723195/

Mirowski, Philip. 2013. *Never Let a Serious Crisis Go to Waste: How Neoliberalism Survived the Financial Meltdown*. Verso.

Mishra, Pankaj. 2017. *Age of Anger: A History of the Present*. Allen Lane.

Moffitt, Benjamin. 2016. *The Global Rise of Populism: Performance, Political Style, and Representation*. Stanford University Press.

Mont Pelerin Society. 1947. Statement of aims. Mont Pelerin, Switzerland, 8 April 1947. Accessed 01 Oct 2024: www.montpelerin.org/Statement-of-Aims.html

Mouffe, Chantal. 2005. *On the Political*. Routledge.

Mouffe, Chantal. 2018. *For a Left Populism*. Verso Books.

Mounk, Yascha and Kyle, Jordan. 2018. What populists do to democracies. *The Atlantic* 26 December 2018. Accessed 01 Oct 2024: www.theatlantic.com/ideas/archive/2018/12/hard-data-populism-bolsonaro-trump/578878/

Mudde, Cas and Kaltwasser, Cristóbal Rovira. 2017. *Populism: A Very Short Introduction*. Oxford University Press.

Muntean, Pete. 2020. Airspace now restricted over Biden's home. *CNN* 6 November 2020. Accessed 01 Oct 2024: https://edition.cnn.com/politics/live-news/trump-biden-election-results-11-06-20/h_8cd2333f39a78ee9080a7 53e0433035a

Neal, Mark Anthony. 2022. Black masculinity and the slap heard round the world. Interview by Melissa Harris-Perry. *WNYC Studios: The Takeaway* 29 March 2022. Accessed 01 Oct 2024: www.wnycstudios.org/podcasts/takeaway/segments/what-slap-revealed-about-black-masculinity

Neilson, Brett and Rossiter, Ned. 2008. Precarity as a political concept, or, Fordism as exception. *Theory, Culture, and Society* 25(7–8): 51–72.

Nettleingham, David. 2017. Canonical generations and the British Left: The narrative construction of the miners' strike 1984–85. *Sociology* 51(4): 850–864.

Neville-Shepard, Meredith. 2023. "Better never means better for everyone": White feminist necropolitics and Hulu's The Handmaid's Tale. *Quarterly Journal of Speech* 109(1): 2–25.

Ngai, Sianne. 2005. *Ugly Feelings*. Harvard University Press.

Norris, Pippa and Inglehart, Ronald. 2019. *Cultural Backlash: Trump, Brexit, and Authoritarian Populism*. Cambridge University Press.

Nugent, Walter. 2009. *Progressivism: A Very Short Introduction*. Oxford University Press.

Obama, Barack. 2013. Inaugural address by President Barack Obama *The White House* 21 January 2013. Accessed 01 Oct 2024: https://obamawhitehouse.archives.gov/the-press-office/2013/01/21/inaugural-address-president-barack-obama\

Obama, Barack. 2016. Final address to the UN Assembly, 20 September 2016. Accessed 01 Oct 2024: https://time.com/4501910/president-obama-united-nations-speech-transcript/

Oremus, Will. 2016. Stop calling everything "Fake News". *Slate* 6 December 2016. Accessed 01 Oct 2024: https://slate.com/technology/2016/12/stop-calling-everything-fake-news.html

Orgad, Shani and Gill, Rosalind. 2022. *Confidence Culture*. Duke University Press.

Orwell, George. 1937. *The Road to Wigan Peer*. Victor Gollancz.

Oxford Languages. 2016. Oxford Word of the Year 2016. Accessed 01 Oct 2024: https://languages.oup.com/word-of-the-year/2016/

Paasonen, Susanna. 2020. Distracted present, golden past. *Media Theory* 4(2): 11–32.

Packer, George. 2013. *The Unwinding: An Inner History of the New America*. Ferrar, Straus, and Geroux.

Packer, George. 2021. *Last Best Hope: America in Crisis and Renewal*. Random House.

Palmer, Tyrone S. 2017. "What feels more than feeling?": Theorizing the unthinkability of black affect. *Critical Ethnic Studies* 3(2): 31–56.

Paul, Pamela. 2023. Opinion: Progressives aren't liberal. *The New York Times* 16 November 2023. Accessed 01 Oct 2024: www.nytimes.com/2023/11/16/opinion/liberals-and-progressives.html

Peck, Jamie and Theodore, Nik. 2019. Still neoliberalism? *South Atlantic Quarterly* 118(2): 245–265.

Pedwell, Carolyn. 2014. *Affective Relations: The Transnational Politics of Empathy*. Palgrave Macmillan.

Peterson, Jordan B. 2018. *Political Correctness Gone Mad?* Oneworld Publications.

Pew Research Centre. 2021a. The Democratic coalition: A snapshot. Accessed 01 Oct 2024: www.pewresearch.org/politics/2021/11/09/the-democratic-coalition/pp_2021-11-09_political-typology_02-01/

Pew Research Centre. 2021b. Political typology. Accessed 01 Oct 2024: www.pewresearch.org/topic/politics-policy/political-parties-polarization/political-typology/

Phillips, Morgan. 2024. AOC and the squad under fire for not being 'progressive enough' as they squarely support President Biden's reelection. *Daily Mail* 13 July 2024. Accessed 01 Oct 2024: www.dailymail.co.uk/news/article-13628799/aoc-squad-progressives-biden.html

Piketty, Thomas. 2013. *Capital in the Twenty-First Century*. Harvard University Press.

Povinelli, Elizabeth A. 2002. *The Cunning of Recognition. Indigenous Alterities and the Making of Australian Multiculturalism.* Duke University Press.

Povinelli, Elizabeth A. 2021. *Between Gaia and Ground: Four Axioms of Existence and the Ancestral Catastrophe of Late Liberalism.* Duke University Press.

Quinn, Ben. 2024. Farage says he is part of 'similar phenomenon' to Andrew Tate among young men. *The Guardian* 3 July 2024. Accessed 01 Oct 2024: www.theguardian.com/politics/article/2024/jul/03/farage-says-he-is-part-of-similar-phenomenon-to-andrew-tate-among-young-men

Ratcliffe, Susan, ed. 2017. *Oxford Essential Quotations* (5th edition). Oxford University Press. Accessed 01 Oct 2024: www.oxfordreference.com/display/10.1093/acref/9780191843730.001.0001/acref-9780191843730

Rawlinson, Kevin. 2024. Stunts, sewage and serious messaging: Lib Dems hope to capitalise on outrage at water pollution *The Guardian* 28 May 2024. Accessed 01 Oct 2024: www.theguardian.com/politics/article/2024/may/28/stunts-sewage-and-serious-messaging-lib-dems-hope-to-capitalise-on-outrage-at-water-pollution

Ray, Sarah Jaquette. 2021. Climate anxiety is an overwhelmingly white phenomenon. *Scientific American* 21 March 2021. Accessed 01 Oct 2024: www.scientificamerican.com/article/the-unbearable-whiteness-of-climate-anxiety/

Relma, Eliza, Seddiq, Oma, and Lahut, Jake. 2021. Trump tells his violent supporters who stormed the Capitol 'you're very special,' but asks them 'to go home.' *Business Insider* 6 January 2021. Accessed 01 Oct 2024: www.businessinsider.com/trump-video-statement-capitol-rioters-we-love-you-very-special-2021-1

Robinson, Emily. 2017. *The Language of Progressive Politics in Modern Britain.* Palgrave Macmillan.

Robson, Amy. 2024. Before it's too late: The extinction script, multi-species reproductive futurism and extinction rebellion. *Transaction of the Institute of British Geographers* (forthcoming).

Roitman, Janet. 2013. *Anti-Crisis.* Duke University Press.

Rose, Nikolas, O'Malley, Pat and Valverde. Mariana. 2006. Governmentality. *Annual Review of Law and Social Science* 2: 83–104.

Rosenthal, Lawrence. 2020. *Empire of Resentment: Populism's Toxic Embrace of Nationalism.* The New Press.

Salter, Leon. 2016. Populism as a fantasmatic rupture in the post-political order: integrating Laclau with Glynos and Stavrakakis. *Kōtuitui: New Zealand Journal of Social Sciences Online* 11(2): 116–132.

Schaffer, Michael. 2022. Joe Biden's 'cardboard box' presidency. *Politico* 8 April 2022. Accessed 01 Oct 2024: www.politico.com/news/magazine/2022/04/08/joe-bidens-boring-presidency-00023923

Schlesinger, Arthur M. Jr. 1948. Not left, not right, but a vital center. *The New York Times* 4 April 1948. Accessed 01 Oct 2024: https://archive.nytimes.com/www.nytimes.com/books/00/11/26/specials/schlesinger-centermag.html?module=inline

Schram, Sanford. 2015. *The Return of Ordinary Capitalism: Neoliberalism, Precarity, Occupy*. Oxford University Press.

Scothorne, Rory. 2022. The man without qualities: Why Keir Starmer can't afford not to have a political vision. *The New Statesman* 25 January 2022. Accessed 01 Oct 2024: www.newstatesman.com/ideas/2022/01/the-man-without-qualities-why-keir-starmer-cant-afford-not-to-have-a-political-vision

Secor, Anna J. and Anderson, Ben. 2024. Affect and ideology. *New Formations* 112: 4–15.

Secor, Anna J. and Blum, Virgina. 2023. Lockdown time, time loops, and the crisis of the future. *Psychoanalysis, Culture & Society* 28(2): 250–267.

Secor, Anna J., Ruez, Derek, Cockayne, Daniel. 2024. Love and work: Affect and ideology beyond the "Great Resignation". *New Formations* 112: 84–112.

Sedgwick, Eve. 2003. *Touching Feeling: Affect, Pedagogy, Performativity*. Duke University Press.

Serwer, Adam. 2018. The cruelty is the point. *The Atlantic* 3 October 2018. Accessed 01 Oct 2024: www.theatlantic.com/ideas/archive/2018/10/the-cruelty-is-the-point/572104/

Seymour, Richard. 2012. *The Liberal Defence of Murder*. Verso.

Shepherd, Brittany. 2020. It just won't be so exhausting: Obama debuts his closing argument for Biden. *Yahoo!News* 22 October 2020. Accessed 01 Oct 2024: https://shorturl.at/CfK2M

Shotwell, Alexis. 2016. *Against Purity: Living Ethically in Compromised Times*. University of Minnesota Press.

References

Seigworth, Gregory J. and Pedwell, Carolyn. 2023. Introduction: A shimmer of inventories. In *The Affect Theory Reader 2: Worldings, Tensions, Futures*, ed. Gregory J. Seigworth and Carolyn Pedwell, 1–59. Duke University Press.

Silva, Jennifer M. 2013. *Coming Up Short: Working-Class Adulthood in an Age of Uncertainty.* Oxford University Press.

Smith, J.A. 2019. *Other People's Politics: Populism to Corbynism.* Zero Books.

Solnit, Rebecca and Lutunatabua, Thelma 2023. *Not Too Late: Changing the Climate Story from Despair to Possibility.* Haymarket Books.

Starmer, Keir. 2023. Keir Starmer's speech at Labour Conference. *Labour.org* 10 October 2023. Accessed 01 Oct 2024: https://labour.org.uk/updates/press-releases/keir-starmers-speech-at-labour-conference/

Starmer, Keir. 2024. Sir Keir Starmer says 'snake oil charm' of populism is a dead end for the UK – video. *Daily Record* 17 July 2024. Accessed 01 Oct 2024: www.youtube.com/watch?v=N-hlzZmJAOo

Stavrakakis, Yannis. 2007. *Lacanian Left.* Edinburgh University Press.

Stewart, Heather. 2022. Stop calling me boring, Keir Starmer tells shadow cabinet. *The Guardian* 14 June 2022. Accessed 01 Oct 2024: www.theguardian.com/politics/2022/jun/14/stop-calling-me-boring-keir-starmer-tells-shadow-cabinet

Stewart, Kathleen. 2017. *Ordinary Affects.* Duke University Press.

Swyngedow, Eric. 2019. The perverse lure of autocratic postdemocracy. *South Atlantic Quarterly* 118(2): 267–286.

Tan, Rebecca, Schmidt, Samantha, Miller, Michael, and Contrera, Jessica. 2020. Before Trump vows to end 'lawlessness', federal officers confront protesters outside White House. *The Washington Post* 2 June 2020. Accessed 01 Oct 2024: www.washingtonpost.com/local/washington-dc-protest-white-house-george-floyd/2020/06/01/6b193d1c-a3c9-11ea-bb20-ebf0921f3bbd_story.html

Taylor, Faith MacNeil. 2021. Cumulative precarity: Millennial experience and multigenerational cohabitation in Hackney, London. *Antipode* 53(2): 587–606.

Taylor, Faith MacNeil. 2024. *Precarious Intimacies: Generation, Rent and the Reproduction of Relationships in London.* Bristol University Press.

Thorkelson, Eli. 2016. Precarity outside: The political unconscious of French academic labor. *American Ethnologist* 43(3): 475–487.

Thunberg, Greta. 2019. Address at World Economic Forum: Our house is on fire. 19. January 2019. Accessed 01 Oct 2024: https://awpc.cattcenter.iastate.edu/2019/12/02/address-at-davos-our-house-is-on-fire-jan-25-2019/

Trump, Donald J. 2016. Donald Trump's argument for America. *Team Trump* 6 November 2016. Accessed 01 Oct 2024: www.youtube.com/watch?v=vST61W4bGm8

Trump, Donald J. 2017. The inaugural address. Accessed 01 Oct 2024: www.politico.com/story/2017/01/full-text-donald-trump-inauguration-speech-transcript-233907

Trump, Donald J. 2020. White House conference. Accessed 01 Oct 2024: www.whitehouse.gov/briefings-statements/remarks-president-trump-white-house-conference-american-history/

Trump, Donald J. 2024a. Trump claims he's taken 'more wounds' than any other president at DC faith conference – video. *Independent* 22 June 2024. Accessed 01 Oct 2024: www.independent.co.uk/tv/news/faith-and-freedom-trump-wounds-dc-b2567189.html

Trump, Donald J. 2024b. President Trump in Las Vegas. Donald J. Trump 9 June 2024. Accessed 01 Oct 2024: www.youtube.com/watch?v=XpLxd2_JkP4

Trump, Donald J. 2024c. Donald Trump's full speech at the RNC – video. *ABC News* 19 June 2024 Accessed 01 Oct 2024: www.youtube.com/watch?v=ibjf6anX7c0

Tsing, Anna. 2015. *The Mushroom at the End of the World: On the Possibility of Life in Capitalist Ruins.* Princeton University Press.

Ulloa, Jazmine and Lerer, Lisa. 2023. For progressive democrats, new momentum clashes with old debates. *The New York Times* 19 April 2023. Accessed 01 Oct 2024: www.nytimes.com/2023/04/19/us/politics/progressives-moderates-democrats.html?searchResultPosition=4

Wacquant, Loic. 2009. *Punishing the Poor: The Neoliberal Government of Social Insecurity.* Duke University Press.

Warren, Calvin. 2018. *Ontological Terror: Blackness, Nihilism, and Emancipation.* Duke University Press.

Whannel, Kate. 2024. Farage challenged over canvasser's racist slurs. *BBC News* 28 June 2024. Accessed 01 Oct 2024: www.bbc.co.uk/news/articles/cgxq82xwkl1o

Wilkie, Christina. 2020. Republican National Convention kicks off with a near spiritual devotion to Trump. CNBC 25 August 2020. Accessed 01 Oct 2024: www.cnbc.com/2020/08/25/rnc-kicks-off-near-spiritual-devotion-to-trump.html

Williams, Raymond. 1958. *Culture and Society, 1780–1950*. Penguin Books.

Williams, Raymond. 1973. *The Country and the City*. Spokesman Books.

Williams, Raymond. 1977. *Marxism and Literature*. Oxford University Press.

Wilson, Julie A. and Yochim, Emily A. Chivers. 2017. *Mothering Through Precarity: Women's Work and Digital Media*. Duke University Press.

Winnicott, Donald W. 1974. Fear of breakdown. In *Psychoanalytic Explorations*, ed. C. Winnicott, R. Shepherd, and M. Davis, 87–95. Harvard University Press.

Woodcock, Andrew. 2022. Starmer says birth of children, not bungee jump, was his 'most exciting moment'. *Independent* 28 September 2022. Accessed 01 Oct 2024: www.independent.co.uk/news/uk/politics/keir-starmer-children-labour-conference-b2177010.html

Wynter, Sylvia. 2003. Unsettling the coloniality of being/power/truth/freedom: Towards the human, after man, its overrepresentation – an argument. *CR: The New Centennial Review* 3(3): 257–337.

Yao, Xine. 2021. *Disaffected: The Cultural Politics of Unfeeling in Nineteenth-Century America*. Duke University Press.

YouGov. 2012. *Public Understandings of Progressive*. Presentation by Joe Twyman. Accessed 01 Oct 2024: https://d3nkl3psvxxpe9.cloudfront.net/documents/progressive_conference_sendout_WithResults_HT.pdf

Žižek, Slavoj. 2002. *For They Know Not What They Do: Enjoyment as a Political Factor*. Verso.

Index

#MeToo, 10, 66

Absolution, 44, 66
Affect, 3-4, 7, 51, 111, 113, 128, 135
   and 'alien', 22, 61
   and appeal, 3, 6, 26, 30n8, 40, 42, 58-59, 64
   and differentiation, 24
   and ideology, 13-19
   and politics, 5
   and presence, 38, 40
   and racialised, 4, 31, 49, 51, 80
   and theory, 16, 16n2, 39
   and white, 45, 101, 119, 126, 136
Affirmation, 44, 56-63, 65, 68, 90, 103, 105
Ahmed, Sara, 22, 61
Alderman, Naomi, 93, 128
Allure, 11-12, 20, 40, 42, 188
Ambiguity, 24, 34, 42-43, 50
Ambivalence, 34, 40, 53, 70. 81, 165, 188
   and Berlant, 86n4
   unambivalence, 45, 85, 113, 188
American Dream, 32, 35, 80, 80n2, 170
Anger, 3, 168, 177-178, 186;
   'age of', 25, 56
   and Black Lives Matter, 10
   and 'left behind', 51, 179
   and liberalism, 153-154
   and Palestine, 22
   or rage, 20, 70
   and right-wing populism, 56, 64, 65-68, 70, 74-75, 180
Another world is possible, slogan, 96, 110-111

Anxiety, 22, 29, 35, 37-38, 51, 116-117, 119, 125, 169
   and climate, 125-126
Apocalyptic politics, 34, 101, 111, 118, 127. *See also* catastrophe
Atmosphere, 13, 19, 21, 28, 32, 55, 73, 101-102, 124, 143, 150
Attachment, 2-4, 12, 15, 18, 46, 78, 80-81, 83-87, 90-91, 100-101, 133, 154, 156, 160, 177, 180-181, 185
   crisis of, 46, 103, 135-136, 148-151, 161
   to EU, 157-159
   and problematic, 29, 34, 81, 85, 104-106
   or reattachment, 44, 157
   and weak or fragile, 11, 85, 105-106, 177
   and work, 29, 30n9. *See also* Berlant, Lauren
Atwood, Margaret, 115-117
Austerity, 7, 150
Authoritarianism 76, 95-96, 108-109, 137
   and neoliberalism 6, 134, 152
   and populism, 15, 25, 55, 65, 71, 137, 168

Bannon, Steve, 134, 154
Bellicosity, 8, 45, 49, 66, 68-69, 79, 82, 153, 172-173, 177, 180
Benjamin, Walter, 106-107, 153
Berlant, Lauren, 16, 16n2, 24, 29, 34, 43, 81, 84-87, 86n4, 89
Biden, Joe, 1, 9, 67-68, 74, 78, 101, 161-163, 166, 170, 187

Index

Black Lives Matter 1, 10, 36, 66, 79, 85, 119, 173
Boredom 2, 13, 21, 39, 49
 and liberalism, 163–167
Brexit, 5, 8–9, 53, 59, 66, 72, 87, 97, 128, 133, 156–159, 162, 173, 179
Brown, Gordon, 58
Brown, Wendy, 44, 56, 58, 65–66, 150, 152–153, 178–179

Capitalism, 7, 12, 31, 36–37, 143, 150, 152
Catastrophe, 3, 35, 44–45, 96, 102, 106–107, 113–119, 123–129, 151, 169. *See also* apocalyptic politics
Centrist dad, 160
Change, 1–2, 7–8, 37, 46, 95, 104, 113
 and crisis, 6, 10
 no need for, 160–174
Climate change, 33, 103, 113–114, 124–125, 125n5
Clinton, Bill, 132, 135, 136
Clinton, Hilary, 57–58, 63, 68, 128, 132
Colebrook, Claire, 118, 127
Colonialism, 35, 81, 99, 115, 119, 127, 141
 or decolonial, 119
 or post-colonial, 80, 81, 83, 126
Common sense, 9–11, 15, 23–24, 90, 143–144, 148–149, 159, 165
 cracking of, 11, 168, 175, 177, 185
 and liberal, 14, 45–46, 133–135, 180, 181
 and neoliberal, 177, 179, 185
Competitive individualism, 12
Confusion, 13, 166, 173
Conjuncture, 1, 6, 15, 51, 113, 185, 189
Corbyn, Jeremy, 8, 104, 154, 162, 178
COVID-19, 9, 15, 79, 103, 112, 170
Crisis, 1–2, 5–7, 9–13, 16, 18, 24–25, 28, 32–38, 40–41, 43–47, 49–51, 58, 70, 73, 95, 102–103, 110, 112–113, 124–125, 128, 131, 133–136, 138, 148, 152, 161, 163, 167–170, 172–173, 176–179, 181–182, 185–187, 189
 of attachment, 46, 135–136, 148
 climate change, 32–33
 of collapsing promises, 13
 conjunctural crisis, 5–13, 18, 24–25, 38, 47, 95, 134, 168, 176–177, 182, 185, 186
 cost-of-living, 32
 environmental, 96, 124
 and everyday/everyday life, 32–33
 financial, 1–2, 6–7, 9, 24, 50–51, 152, 177
 of the future, 70
 of intimacy and recognition, 12
 of liberalism, 134
 neoliberal crisis, 16
 and normality, 103
 polycrisis, 32
 and precarity, 31, 40–41
 of the present, 181
 of response, 49
Cruel Optimism, 81, 83. *See also* Berlant, Lauren
Culture war, 79–80, 85
Cummings, Dominic, 134, 154

Democracy, 70–71, 77, 97, 133, 135, 137, 139, 149
Detachment, 12, 46, 105–106, 115, 122, 142, 161, 164–165, 168, 172, 186
Diagnostic critique, 4, 25, 188
Difference, 10, 19–24, 56–57, 69, 178
 of liberalism, 131
 of populism, 72
Differentiation, 20, 24, 111, 125, 183, 187
Disaffection, 1, 13, 18, 21, 44, 91, 126, 178, 183–184. *See also* Yao, Xine
Disaffected consent, 126, 135, 167

Index

Dispossession, 28, 35, 65, 107, 114, 133, 168
Disruption, 83, 88, 141, 171
Dissolution, 85
Dullness dividend, 162, 168

Elite, 7, 23, 29, 44, 52, 62–63, 65–66, 83–84, 142, 180
  establishment, 44, 59, 62–63, 65–66, 69, 180
Emergency, 3, 59, 66, 69, 124–125, 151, 179
  emergent, 5, 7, 18, 23, 36, 40, 51–52, 54, 88, 91, 124, 187
  pre-emergent, 5, 18, 36
Enjoyment, 3, 30, 46, 69, 75–78, 84, 89, 143, 154, 169, 183
European Union, 53, 87, 132
Event, 7–9, 32–33, 38, 46, 72, 79, 89, 120, 122, 132, 147, 159, 183, 187
Excess, 10, 30, 44, 51, 57, 64, 68–78, 84, 89–90, 118, 152, 161–162, 166
  excessiveness, 72, 85, 88, 99
Exhilaration, 3

Fantasy, 85, 87, 116, 123, 128, 188
  fantasies, 12, 31, 35, 71, 81, 85–87, 89, 127, 179
  good life, 12, 31, 35, 81, 85–86
Farage, Nigel, 1, 20, 53–54, 59, 61, 66–69, 76, 147
Feminist, 22, 36, 61, 93, 117
  femininity, 23
Financial crisis 2008, 1–2, 6–7, 24, 36, 50, 51, 58, 152, 177
Fisher, Mark, 11, 34, 135, 143, 178
Fordism, 7, 11, 30–31, 34, 81, 85, 87, 104–105
  Fordist-Keynesian, 7, 11, 31, 34
Fragments, 60, 107, 109–110, 125, 127, 151, 176, 181
  of the past, 107, 109–110, 127
Freedom, 12, 30, 36, 74, 76, 108, 133, 137–138, 144–145, 169, 181

Fukuyama, Francis, 14, 136–140, 146–148, 164–165, 169
Fun, 49, 64, 68–69, 73, 180, 188
Future, 1, 6, 9, 11, 31–41, 44–45, 50, 57, 78, 81–90, 93–97, 100–102, 105–107, 109–111, 113–119, 121, 123–125, 127–128, 132–133, 135, 137–139, 141–142, 145, 150–151, 153, 159–160, 163, 168–172, 174, 176, 179–182
  of America, 1, 86, 145
  bad future, 45, 111, 113, 117, 137, 169, 181
  catastrophic future, 34, 96, 101, 111, 115–116, 160, 167, 186
  climate changed future, 96, 125
  future dystopia, 117
  futures, 5, 11, 34, 36, 41, 44, 57, 76, 83, 85, 88, 90, 96, 107, 109, 114, 116, 167, 185–186
  futurism, 34, 117
  good future, 31, 127–128, 171
  insecure futures, 104
  lost futures, 90, 101
  multiple futures, 10, 32, 26
  no future, 34, 36
  past futures, 36, 107, 109–110
  relations with past and present, 36, 93, 101
  and security, 1, 31–32, 104, 169

Gilbert, Jeremy, 24–25, 37, 61, 135, 177–178
Growth, 1, 11, 13, 30, 55, 104, 162, 169–170, 172, 176

Hall, Stuart, 5–6, 9–10, 25, 43, 188
Hegemony, 5, 13, 15, 28, 40, 45, 140, 177
  hegemonic, 6, 14, 30, 36, 76–77, 84, 135, 177
  neoliberal hegemony, 13, 40, 177
Hogan, Hulk, 175, 180

Hope, 13, 42–43, 46–47, 51, 55, 87, 97, 101, 104, 107, 109–113, 124–125, 128, 135–136, 142–148, 150, 153, 156, 158–159, 162, 164, 170–173, 180–181, 183–184, 186–187, 189
   act of hope, 124
   and despair, 13, 37, 101, 181
   desperate hope, 147–148
   fragile hope, 124, 187
   hope of return to a near past, 173
   hopeful, 99, 123–125
   hopeless, 110
   keeping hope alive, 107, 109
   negative hope, 159
   progressive hope, 110, 112
   possibility of another world, 111, 127
   progressive hope, 110, 112
   shrinking hope, 51
   weak hope, 46, 110, 136, 181

Identification, 12, 60, 76
Ideology, 4–5, 9–10, 13–18, 22–23, 49, 94, 123, 139, 142, 181–182, 185
   ideological systems, 2, 9, 14–15, 17, 21, 23, 177
   ideologies, 2, 4, 16, 23, 94
Immigrant, 1, 53, 58–59, 66–69, 77
   anti-immigrant, 53, 58–59, 66–69, 77
Impasse, 1–2, 4, 8–9, 12, 27, 43, 45–46, 72, 78, 100–101, 111, 114, 123, 127, 129, 134, 143, 157–158, 169, 177, 181, 186
   Brexit impasse, 72
   and events, 9, 72, 157
   extended impasse, 2, 9
   political impasse, 2, 43
   of progressivism, 169
   stuckness, 33, 150, 159–160
Injury, 63–65
Insecurity, 1, 25, 30–32, 37, 41, 166, 169, 185
Intensity, 3–6, 10, 24, 38–39, 41, 44, 47, 49, 53, 60, 71, 73, 91, 102, 114, 118, 126–127, 129, 134–135, 144, 146–147, 149, 151, 154, 161–162, 164–167, 171, 175, 177–178, 181, 183–184, 186–187
Irrational, 70, 74, 168, 173

Johnson, Boris, 53–55, 71–73, 78, 162

Kettle-logic, 118–119

Left-behind, 30, 51, 65, 78, 106, 134, 141–142, 149, 151, 153, 168, 177
Legitimacy, 4, 11, 28, 134–135, 143, 177
   legitimation, 143
Long 90s, 152, 169

'Make America Great Again', 1, 8, 58, 132, 175, 185
Malatino, Hil, 126
Masculinity, 10, 12, 23, 30, 32, 44, 59, 121–122, 147, 160, 180
   Masculinism, 65, 77, 183
   Masculinist, 23, 151
Massumi, Brian, 16, 52, 156
Mediation, 8, 12, 37, 39–40, 155, 185
Melancholy, 46, 135, 148, 160, 164, 172
   left melancholia, 150–153
   liberal melancholia, 135, 153, 156, 173
   melodrama, 122–123
   postcolonial and postimperial melancholia, 80, 83
Meme, 38–39, 52, 112, 120, 160, 176
   memescape, 53
Meritocracy, 12, 34, 141
   Meritocratic, 142, 149
Middle class, 7, 13, 29, 35, 117–118, 126, 185
Miners, strike 1984–1985, 108, 108n2, 109, 110
Minor feelings, 22–23, 184

Index

Modernity, 34, 88, 95, 97–98, 107, 149
Mont Pelerin Society, 144–145

Neoliberal, 1, 6–7, 11–13, 16, 24, 28, 34, 40, 44, 50, 62, 104, 135, 139, 152, 166, 177–178, 185
  neoliberal capitalism, 7
  Neoliberalism, 4, 6, 11–13, 28, 40, 50, 132–135, 137, 144–145, 150–152, 178–179
Ngai, Sianne, 22
Nihilism, 8, 34, 36, 107, 178
Non-linear time, 16, 33–36, 84, 88, 106, 110, 141–142, 170
Nostalgia, 8, 28, 31, 38, 83, 104–105, 152, 169

Obama, Barak, 99–100, 105–106, 132, 138–141, 146, 149, 161–162
Optimism, 8, 36, 44–45, 57, 81–86, 88–90, 97, 112–113, 149, 152, 159, 166, 168, 170, 175, 188
  cruel, 81, 83, 86
  time-loop, 44–45, 175
Other/Othering, 65–66
Outrage, 3, 13, 19, 37–39, 53, 79, 170, 179

Palestine, 22, 101
  Palestinian, 22, 66, 154
Pandemic, 15, 21, 46, 79, 96, 112–113
Passion, 19, 69–70, 73–74, 76–78, 91, 99, 114, 146, 158, 173
  passionate, 12, 76, 146–147, 149, 161, 178, 181
Past, 4–5, 9, 13, 17, 24, 30, 34–36, 41–42, 44–45, 50, 53, 61, 66, 78–79, 81–89, 95, 100–107, 109–114, 117–119, 123, 125, 127, 132, 135, 138–139, 141, 148–153, 156–157, 159–162, 167–170, 172–174, 179–182
  available, 103
  bad past, 107, 110–111, 114, 127
  far past/distant past, 82
  fragment/fragments of good past, 109
  good liberal near-past, 152
  good past, 83, 107, 109, 113, 180–181
  impasse between past and future, 123
  nationalist past, 179
  not-quite lost/almost lost past, 34, 44, 80, 88, 103, 107, 156
  past attachments, 81
  past futures, 34, 36, 107, 109
  past of progress, 127, 141
  past promissory objects, 61
  with present and future, 34, 82, 84, 101
  past presents, 83
  return to a better past, 87, 105
  unproblematic past, 104–105
  wreckage of, 102, 107
People, the, 26, 52, 55, 57, 63–66, 75, 77, 82–83, 85, 88, 90, 158
Platform capitalism, 14, 30, 37
Polarisation, 7, 21, 24, 160
Post-truth, 52, 132, 134, 154–157, 159, 166, 184
Post-war settlement, 31, 81, 87, 104
Povinelli, Elizabeth, 64, 115, 117
Precarity, 28–32, 37, 40–41, 59, 102, 104, 166–167
  precarious, 8, 28–31, 106, 118, 124, 138, 146
  precariousness, 5, 28–33, 96, 102, 124, 170, 180
Present, 1–13, 15, 17–19, 22, 24–27, 29, 31–46, 50, 54–56, 62–63, 78, 81–88, 90, 95–96, 99–106, 108–111, 113–115, 118–119, 122–128, 131–132, 134, 136, 138–143, 146–152, 154, 156–157, 161, 163–164, 166–167, 169–186, 188
  digitally mediated present, 6, 37, 39–40, 52–53, 156, 186
  intense present, 163

Progress, 35–36, 45, 76, 84, 87–88, 93–96, 98–101, 104, 106–107, 110–111, 113, 123, 127–129, 131, 135, 138–143, 148, 150, 156, 164, 170, 173–174, 180–181
  progressive betterment, 33, 35, 41, 81
Promise, 1, 4, 12–13, 28–29, 31–33, 41, 43–46, 55, 59, 61, 67–68, 71–72, 78, 83–84, 86–87, 95–96, 99, 101, 104–105, 110, 123, 127–128, 132, 135–136, 139, 141–142, 154, 156, 159, 161–163, 165–174, 177, 180, 183, 188
  affirmation and recognition, 56–63, 65, 68, 75, 105
  collapsing promises, 13
  the disappearance of politics, 173
  exhausted promises,
  holding onto, 29
  of meritocracy 12, 141
  nothing ever need change, 46, 136
  passionate intensity, 146–147, 161, 181
  of whiteness, 79, 84
Propositions, 6, 40, 42–43, 47, 53, 55–56, 88–90, 101, 180, 182, 186–189
Public Mood, 1
  mood, 1, 3, 45, 138, 143, 148, 184

Queer theory/theories, 39

Racialisation, 23, 31, 31, 44, 49, 51, 71, 80, 126, 180
  racism, 21, 75, 80, 119, 121, 126, 133, 171
  racist, 58, 75–76, 98–99, 178
Recognition 12, 44, 56–61, 63–66, 69, 82–84, 164, 180, 187
  un-recognised (mis-recognised), 58–59, 64
Resentment, 3, 44–45, 49, 51, 60, 64–65, 67–68, 82, 108, 153–154, 168
  racialised, 31, 44, 49, 51, 180

Residual, 7, 18, 31, 42, 81, 104, 157
Resolution, 4, 6, 9, 41, 87, 162, 186
Responsibility, 41, 62–63, 119, 123, 156, 187
  responsibilisation, 44, 62
Rupture, 6–7, 34, 88, 94, 103, 110, 113, 151, 173, 179

Sanders, Bernie, 1, 8, 178
Security, 29–30, 32, 67, 104, 138
Settlement, 6–8, 11, 30–31, 34, 40, 81, 85, 87, 104
Shock, 8, 57, 107, 112, 132, 138, 142, 173, 186
Slow cancellation of the future, 33–34, 36, 41, 57, 81
Spirit of 1989, 148, 150, 161
Starmer, Keir, 162–163, 166–171, 176–177
State phobia, 7, 144
Structure of feeling, 11, 13, 20, 34, 37, 42, 45, 50, 52, 55–57, 70, 75–77, 90, 94, 96, 100, 107, 111, 113, 126–128, 136, 143, 149, 151, 172–173, 181
Sunak, Rishi, 73, 76, 162, 166
Surprise, 8, 51, 81

Take Back Control, 1, 132
Temporality, 35, 38, 84, 114, 180
  non-linear, 110
  time-loop, 8, 45, 85, 182
Tendency/Tendencies, 5–6, 13, 16, 27, 40, 42, 89, 95, 99, 139, 144, 184–185
Thatcher, Margaret, 11, 108
  Thatcherism, 15, 25, 152, 188
The Handmaid's Tale, 115–117
There is no alternative, 11, 15, 28, 45, 57–58, 69, 110, 132, 135, 143, 150, 154, 160, 177, 178–179
Threat, 1, 30, 60, 70–71, 75, 82, 113, 131, 136–138, 144–145, 147, 159, 161, 164, 176
Time-Loop Optimism, 45

Index

Blair, Tony, 132, 135–136, 142, 146–147, 149
Trans, 66, 110, 126
  anti-trans, 102, 110
Trump, Donald, 1, 5, 8–9, 15, 22, 39, 41, 46, 49, 51, 53–55, 57–58, 60–64, 67–75, 79–80, 82, 84, 86–87, 89–90, 116, 128, 131–133, 138, 155–156, 161–162, 164, 173, 175–179, 186
  6 January 2021, 15–16, 89
  Trumpian, 50, 68, 131
  Trumpmania, 175
Truth, 46, 52, 79, 132, 134, 147, 154–157, 159–161, 166, 170, 172, 184–185
Turbulent, 157, 167, 181
  turbulence, 2, 5, 9–10, 24, 51, 157, 162, 172, 177–178, 186

Ukraine, 46, 147–148, 163
Uncertainty, 3–4, 11, 24–25, 32, 37, 41, 50, 70, 84, 89, 112, 119, 138, 163, 166, 187

Viral, 73, 115, 120

Whiteness, 8, 12, 30, 79, 84, 111, 114, 119, 126, 149, 153, 160, 172
  detachment, 115, 119
  fears, 126
  feelings, 126
  supremacy, 75, 77, 79, 131, 161, 172
  detachment, 115, 119
  White, 8, 10, 23, 28, 35, 44–46, 51, 54, 59–61, 63, 65, 70, 72, 75–77, 79–80, 90, 98, 101, 114–115, 117–119, 125–126, 128, 131, 136, 142, 151, 153, 161, 171–172, 175–176, 180, 183
Woke, 44, 60, 62–63, 66, 96, 98, 119
  war on woke, 44, 60, 63
Working class, 57, 59, 63, 108, 151
Wounded, 64
  wounded subjectivity, 64

Yao, Xine, 24, 123, 126